CW00847472

From Confusion to Conclusion

How to Write a First-Class Essay

Copyright © 2012 Vlad Mackevic

All rights reserved.

ISBN: 1480041793
ISBN-13: 978-1480041790

From Confusion to Conclusion

How to Write a First-Class Essay

Vlad Mackevic

Edited by Tom Wild

Published in association with

www.FirstYearCounts.com
www.TheLectureRoom.co.uk

Copyright © 2012 by Vlad Mackevic.

PUBLISHED BY: Published by Vlad Mackevic through Amazon's CreateSpace and in association, but no financial affiliation with *First Year Counts* and *The Lecture Room* in 2012.

For any questions about the content of this book or its author, please refer to the contact details at www.FirstYearCounts.com.

Book Cover Design © Vlad Mackevic.

All rights reserved. Without limiting the rights under copyright reserved above, no part of this publication may be reproduced, stored in or introduced into a retrieval system, or transmitted, in any form, or by any means (electronic, mechanical, photocopying, recording, or otherwise) without the prior written permission of both the copyright owners and the above publisher of this book.

The information this book contains is based on the author's personal experience. Please do not assume and hereby disclaim any liability to any party for any loss, damage, or disruption caused by possible differences between the author's experience and that of his readers. Although the author and publisher have made every effort to ensure that the information in this book was correct at press time, the author and publisher do not assume and hereby disclaim any liability to any party for any loss, damage, or disruption caused by errors or omissions, whether such errors or omissions result from negligence, accident, or any other cause.

CONTENTS

Contents

PREFACE

WHY ARE YOU reading this book?

Because you are at university. Because you are a student. Because you have to write an academic assignment. It's as simple as that. It doesn't even matter what kind of assignment it is. What matters is that you want to become better at what you're doing – and I want to thank you for choosing my book on your path to academic success. In this book, I promise to share all I know about essay, exam and dissertation writing.

In 2011, I graduated from Aston University, Birmingham, with a first-class degree in International Relations and English. During my four years at Aston, I worked in the university's Learning Development Centre, teaching my fellow students essay writing skills. During my placement year, I worked as a communications officer for The Science and Technology Facilities Council, spending my days writing promotional materials and my evenings writing a research project for university, as well as short stories (three of which were published in a small literary magazine). During my degree course, I also published three articles on linguistics in *Début: The Undergraduate Journal of Languages, Linguistics and Area Studies*.

In other words, ***I've been there and done that***. I've got the scars, too! I have a lot of writing experience, both at university and outside of it. And here's what I can tell you.

The transition from school to university is not easy. All of a sudden, you're expected to obey all sorts of rules of writing that you had never heard of when you were at school. You have to write following a certain structure and using certain

1

vocabulary; you're not allowed to say 'I think', and you have to reference your work, which can make what you thought would be an expression of your creativity and ability to reason feel like simply repeating the findings of others.

It's not what you expect. It's tough. You have to learn to adapt. To make mistakes and learn through trial and error.

And the toughest part is not the research process or the referencing.

It's always the writing itself.

That's why I'm writing this book: I want to help you become the best without going through what I went through. Without guessing and trying, without hitting and missing. After so many years, I know how university assignments work. Moreover, I know how to *make them work*.

I'm writing this book to make it easier for you to score 10-30% higher in *every* assignment you submit. Yes, I mean it! Because it's nothing but pure technique. The key is to become aware of what you're doing: how you're writing your assignments, what exactly you're doing well and whether there are any areas that need improvement. Once you start consciously applying the methods I outline in this book, you will boost your grades and be a first-class student before you know it.

My Story

Before I begin describing the techniques and giving you all sorts of useful tips, I want to give you some background information about my own academic and personal development.

When I started university, I initially enrolled on a business administration course. I completed a year, got a 70% average (mostly owing to the mathematics-based modules) and then decided it wasn't for me. I didn't like it, didn't feel passionate about it. If I had simply gritted my teeth and carried on, I could have succeeded as a business student, but it would have been a highly stressful three years.

I realised that I could only succeed doing something I felt passionate about – so I changed to International Relations and English. Yet, my love for the subjects was still not enough to get me a first.

In my first year, still on the business course, I faced an issue familiar to every student making the transition from sixth form or college to university: *I had no idea how to write academic assignments*.

I had the ability to memorise facts; I could learn by rote pretty well. Constant practice at school made me good at maths. Still, I knew nothing about the techniques that lead to academic success. Learning by heart was not enough for university.

When it was announced that we would have to submit a portfolio of two essays and ten other written tasks for one of our modules, all 400 first year undergraduate business students panicked. We were all inexperienced. We didn't have a clue about essay writing at university level! How could they expect us to produce dozens of pages of written work?

In order to write a first-class essay, you need more than a thorough knowledge of the subject or perfect grammar. There's something else that is much more important: *a set of tricks and techniques* that can make a good essay into a brilliant one – and which *no one* bothers to teach you at university! Usually, you find out these things when you get a mark that's lower than you expected. You go to your lecturer and they tell you where you went wrong. If you're lucky.

I learnt these tricks and techniques the hard way – and a strange way, too.

One of the best things that happened to me during my year studying business was unexpectedly getting a mark of 84% for my coursework. This helped me get the writing mentor's job in the university library. Yet, when I reflected upon it later, I realised that getting that mark was *sheer luck*. The luck of a novice.

Yes, I did get a high grade. Yes, I did write a good essay. But I had no idea **how to do it again**.

I could correct basic, common-sense mistakes in an essay that needed improvement, but I didn't know how to consistently produce first-rate pieces of work. All I knew was that I had done something that worked and I could only hope that I might do it again.

Moreover, getting a writing mentor's job meant that I had to become an awesome employee – which also meant a great degree of responsibility. I no longer had the luxury of not knowing how first-class academic assignments are produced. So, I began studying my coursework portfolio, examining it from every angle, trying to pick out what I did well, bit by bit. I read books on essay writing and compared my own writing with what they advised.

It took me a long time to pick out all the features that led to my coursework success.

But I got there in the end.

At first, when I changed my degree course, my essay grades were hitting high and low sixties. It was close, but it was never a first. The luck of a novice was gone as well – I only scored over 80% once, in the final year, when I already knew all the tricks of the trade.

I got these marks because I knew the subject, not because I was good at assignment writing. But, as I realised more and more what I had done correctly, I started to apply the techniques I had identified in subsequent essays.

And then it started happening. Towards the second term of my first year studying International Relations and English, I started hitting seventies! Even for lazy, sloppy essays.

I finished university with a first class degree, three academic publications and a great work placement where I could apply my writing skills, under my belt.

In this book, I am going to tell you exactly what I did to succeed as a student without snapping from overwork!

I'll tell you something that you won't usually hear in lecture halls. I'll teach you the techniques that helped me land and keep the writing mentor's job and gave me the chance to pass on my knowledge and teach others what I knew. Once you figure them out, these techniques seem simple, but still, they are not that obvious. And for some reason, most of the time lecturers do not tell you about them.

My academic and professional experience has equipped me with some basic knowledge that everyone should have. That's why I'm sharing it. I want to teach you how to succeed without trying too hard. It will still involve some work, but, if you know what to do and how to do it, it won't feel like hard labour!

Please note, however, that what I'm sharing is subjective. These techniques worked for me, but I cannot guarantee that you will get the same results, or that you will get 70% or more for each assignment if you only apply what I say in this book. A lot depends on your lecturer, specific aspects of your degree subject, the way you approach the assignment, and your own effort. However, I'm sure I can trust you on the last one – after all, if you are reading this book, it means you want to make an effort and succeed, and I am more than happy to help you.

As a writer, I know that writing is hard work. Academic assignments can sometimes feel a bit of a pain in the neck. I just want to make it easier for you. And, since I respect your time, I'll try to do this in about one hundred pages.

Basic knowledge. Pure technique. And some useful examples.

Let's get started!

CHAPTER 1

ACADEMIC WRITING: WHAT DO YOU GET MARKS FOR?

AT UNIVERSITY, YOU get marks for the following elements of your assignment:

- Answering the question
- Structure
- Style and language
- References
- Research and analysis
- Formatting and presentation

These elements are not listed in any order of importance. They are all equally important and every single one of them will earn you points – which all add up and amount to high grades. I will briefly explain each element.

1. Answering the Question

Despite the fact that this sounds obvious, everything you write in your assignment must be done with a sole purpose – answering the question. You have to make it relevant and informative. You must have evidence to back up your claims. The way you answer the question must be logical and coherent. Moreover, you must explain how each paragraph is related to the question or the topic of your assignment.

2. Structure

This is the 'formula' according to which you write your essay, research report or dissertation. It is a special way of organising your writing to make it flow coherently from the introduction to the conclusion. The majority of the chapters in this book deal with the building blocks of academic work – introduction, previous research, methodology, analysis, discussion and conclusion. In subsequent chapters, I will describe each of these, telling you what they consist of and how they should be written to make your academic writing more effective.

3. Style and Language

At university you are expected to write your assignments in 'proper English'. To do this you will need to know the difference between spoken and written language, how to write in appropriate academic style and avoid basic mistakes that make your essay look less professional. You will also need to learn to think and write like an academic.

This, however, does not mean you need to use big words and complicated sentences. Your writing can be plain and simple, and yet very impressive. See **Chapter 12: The Language of Academia** for more information.

4. References

The basic principle of referencing is as follows:

If you write about an idea that you did not come up with yourself, but which was taken from someone else's book or article, you have to give credit to that person and write their name next to the idea.

Referencing is all about respecting the work of others and not stealing someone else's thoughts. You can find more information on referencing in **Chapter 9: Referencing**.

5. Research and Analysis

This differs from subject to subject – so, there is a limit to how much I can help you with this. However, my own experience has taught me that the more you read on your subject, the deeper you will be able to think. ***When you absorb other people's ideas, you generate ideas of your own.***

However, there is one vital aspect of deep analysis: ***being critical.***

This means not believing the first source you read. Read different authors and examine their views on the subject. Are they similar or different? Moreover, how similar are their data and research methods to those you used? It also means acknowledging the limitations of your research. The theory you are using is not the only one; your data will always present a limited picture of the world, and your method is not the only correct one either! For a more in-depth discussion, see **Chapter 7: Analysis and Discussion.**

6. Formatting and Presentation

If you invited your guests to dinner, you wouldn't serve them food on dirty plates.

The same applies to your essay. As your lecturer reads your work, sloppy formatting can be as insulting as a coffee stain across the page. Moreover, formatting usually constitutes five per cent of your mark, so a well-formatted and professionally presented essay can make a difference between a 2:1 and a first!

Make fonts uniform, leave wide margins, double-space your lines and add a conservative cover page – all of this is important. Read more about it in **Chapter 14: Formatting and Presentation.**

CHAPTER 2

THE STRUCTURE OF AN ACADEMIC ASSIGNMENT

THE FIRST THING you need to know about essays and dissertations is that they have a certain structure. There is a formula, a particular order in which academic works are written. Roughly speaking, the formula looks like this:

1. Introduction (10-15% of the word count)
2. Main Body (70-80% of the word count)
3. Conclusion (10-15% of the word count)

These three elements are rudimentary and will be analysed in depth in this book. However, before you begin any analysis, it is important to note **the two main principles on which academic assignments are built.** Depending on the assignment, this can be the *funnel principle* (this looks like a triangle with the tip pointing down) or the *hourglass principle* (two triangles with their tips touching). The diagrams of these principles are presented on the following pages.

2.1. The Funnel and the Hourglass

The *funnel principle* (p. 12) implies a movement from broad to narrow. It is mostly used in academic essays with a set topic (see **Section 2.2.**). First, you describe the theory that is the focus of your essay in general strokes (usually it is the information you find in general textbooks and lecture slides), then you move on to the application of the theory, for example, referring to previous studies (you can find them in academic journals), and finally you examine these studies with a critical eye (your own view of the theory and its applications in relation to your assignment question).

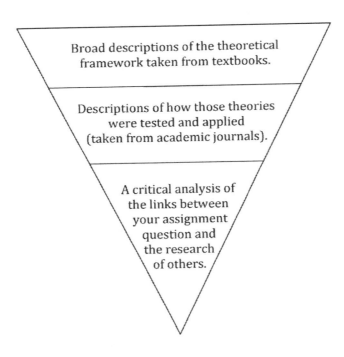

Figure 1: The funnel principle

The ***hourglass principle*** (p. 14) is very different. It usually applies to research assignments with a free topic, where you need to collect certain data and analyse it, such as research reports and dissertations. Your thoughts move from broad to narrow and back to broad again. Moreover, the numbered sections of the hourglass are interlinked.

Section 1 is linked to Section 6 – both discuss theory, but the former gives a broad description of other researchers' theories while the latter focuses on how *your* research has enriched or reinforced the theoretical framework.

Section 2 is linked to Section 5 – both discuss the application of the theory, describing first how it was applied by others, and then discussing your own findings in relation to previous research.

Finally, Section 3 is linked to Section 4, with you describing your data, methods and experiment design and then what you found post-experiment.

Both the funnel and the hourglass primarily reflect the structure of the main body of the assignment. The largest element of your essay, the main body, is made of a number of parts. There are some differences between academic essays with set topics and research papers/reports and dissertations, where you have to create your own research question. This is explained in the next two sections.

2.2. Analysing the Essay Question (Set Questions)

An academic essay is usually a written assignment with a **given (pre-set) topic**. You already know what the topic is – you just need to decipher it through breaking it down into its component parts and answer it.

An essay question is usually made of three parts: the *object* of the study, the *context* of the study and the *method* of the study. Let me explain this, using the following examples.

Example 1

Modern organisations often replace the traditional hierarchical structure with a more 'horizontal' team structure. Select two motivation theories from the field of organisational psychology and discuss how they can be applied in a team-based organisation.

13

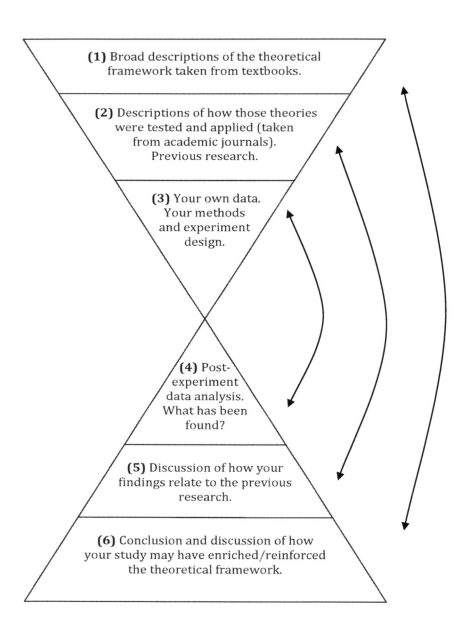

Figure 2: The hourglass principle

This essay question seems really complicated – primarily because the essay title is confusing. You don't know what the object, the context and the method of the study are. You need to *extract* them from the topic and separate them. Let's begin!

The object of the study

The object of your study is something with which you have to perform an *action*. Let's find the action by looking at the verbs in the question. We are only looking for the verbs in the imperative form – those that sound like orders, requests or commands. In this assignment, these words are *select* and *discuss*. Now, what do you need to select? *Two motivation theories.* This is your *object* of study. This is what you are going to analyse. But every kind of analysis needs to be performed in a specific context.

The context of the study

Context means *circumstances*. To find out the context, you need to ask the questions *When? Where? How?* and sometimes, *How much?*

In this essay question, you are not asked to discuss the general application of the two theories. Instead, you are asked to focus on a very specific context – team-based organisations that replace the traditional hierarchical structure with a horizontal team structure. In order to do this, you will naturally have to dedicate one or two paragraphs to describing the context. You will need to tell your reader what it means to have a team-based organisation. You will also need to define hierarchical structure. However, as this is only the context, do not spend too much time on describing it. Although it is very important and often intertwined with the object of the study, it is the background for your writing, but not the topic.

The method of the study

The method of your study is usually an *action*. It is expressed in verbs in the imperative form. As already

15

mentioned these verbs are *select* and *discuss*. *Select* is pretty straightforward. However, *discuss* is more complex. It means look at the context in which the two theories were tested in the past (in hierarchically-structured organisations). Then look at the context of team-based organisations. Then look at the similarities and differences between these two contexts. And finally, based on this, write why these theories can and/or cannot be applied in modern organisations, taking into account all the differences between the traditional hierarchical structure and the team-based structure. Explain why it is possible or not possible each time.

When discussing, think of the following question: *Can the theories you are using be applied under **all** circumstances or not? Or, more broadly, Can **anything** be the case all the time?*

In other words, *discuss* means writing two opposing views and backing them up.

1. It *is* the case because

- Reason A
- Reason B
- Reason C

2. On the other hand, it is *not* the case because

- Reason A
- Reason B
- Reason C

You do not need to have the same number of reasons on both sides. In fact, you can have four reasons for and one against. The main objective is to demonstrate that you know that there are two opposing points of view (because there always are).

Please note that there is a separate section on 'method words' used in essay titles such as *discuss*, giving specific examples and explaining how to understand them in **Chapter 12: The Language of Academia**.

Example 2

What were the reasons for the economic miracle of South Korea in the second half of the twentieth century?

This essay question is pretty straightforward. However, it is worth keeping in mind that even questions like this involve something more than just listing the reasons you have found in the literature. Your lecturers normally expect you to either *present two opposing points of view* or *group your arguments according to certain criteria.*

So, let's start by finding the three elements:

The object of the study

Quite obviously, it is South Korea's economic development.

The context of the study

The context is the time-frame: the second half of the twentieth century. Therefore, you do not need to analyse what happened before this time (unless it led to vital changes in the second half of the twentieth century). Focus on events within the essay time-frame. Don't wander too far away from the essay question.

The method of the study

The method is not expressed as the imperative form of a verb this time. Rather, it is a noun – *reasons*. You need to *find the reasons* – but not just list them in any random order. In an ideal situation, your reasons should be grouped under two slightly opposing categories.

You can usually divide the reasons behind any change into two types: internal and external. It doesn't matter if the change happens at an individual level, the level of an organisation or at a national level.

I am not claiming that this rule is universal, but dividing arguments into two groups, the first involving internal processes in a social group, an organisation, or even a country, and the second related to the external context, is a good start for many assignments that ask you to list reasons.

Example 3

Name the advantages and disadvantages of administering drugs through the skin.

This assignment question is taken from the field of pharmacy/medicine, but a similarly structured question could be found in another area. For example, *What are the benefits and drawbacks of global computerisation?*

Questions like these have no 'yes' or 'no' answer. They have even fewer parts than the previous ones. The **context** of the study is usually implied – it is *now*. You are asked to discuss current events and all your research should be actual rather than historical. Both drug delivery through the skin and global computerisation are happening *now*.

The **object** of the study is also clear – it is drug delivery through the skin in the first question and global computerisation in the second one.

The **method** of the study is finding and naming the advantages and disadvantages. The number of benefits and drawbacks doesn't have to be equal. However, you have to acknowledge that both benefits and drawbacks do exist.

2.3. The Basic Structure of Research Reports and Dissertations

Research reports and dissertations are structured differently from essays. First of all, they do not have a given topic. Normally, you are expected to come up with your own research question. This changes the entire approach to writing because it adds certain elements that are absent from an essay with a set question – but I will deal with this issue in due course.

Listed on the next page are the elements that comprise a research report or a dissertation and where they are covered in this book:

- **Topic or title** – how to create a simple, manageable topic for your research (**Chapter 3**)

- **Introduction** – how to write one and why it's best to write it when you have completed the essay (**Chapter 4**)

- **Literature Review** (also known as 'Previous Research') – why you need one and how to write it (**Chapter 5**)

- **Methodology** – how to collect your data, what research methods you can use and how to use participants in your study (**Chapter 6**)

- **Research** – how you conduct it, what you need to be aware of, quantitative and qualitative research and which research methods are most appropriate (**Chapter 6**)

- **Analysis and Discussion** – what analysis and discussion mean, how you can be critical about your data, why you need to find weaknesses in your research and how you write about them (**Chapter 7**)

- **Conclusion** – how to write a strong ending and leave a long-lasting impression on your readers (**Chapter 8**)

- **References** – why you need to reference and how to do it, with some useful websites with free resources (**Chapter 9**)

These are the basic elements. However, you also need to take into account certain aspects that are common to all academic assignments.

Chapter 10: What About Exams? deals with exam writing strategies. In many disciplines there are so-called 'essay style' exams, where students literally have to write a coherent essay in response to an exam question within a limited amount of time. **Chapter 10** provides tips for successfully passing these exams.

Chapter 11: The Writing Process explains how to make the writing process smoother, covering techniques such as active reading, writing a paragraph, outlining, and brainstorming. It teaches you how to write more efficiently.

Chapter 12: The Language of Academia explains how to understand action words in academic assignments and what the language and style of your essay should be like.

Chapter 13: Writing Tips is a broad discussion of advice on writing. It is made up of three parts:

(1) The Researcher's Point of View gives advice on how to conduct better research, provides resources for research and gives general academic advice.

(2) The Grammarian's Point of View focuses on correct spelling and grammar and lists basic mistakes that you should avoid in your writing.

(3) The Writer's Point of View explains the process of academic writing from a writer's perspective. Writing academic essays is not easy, but the tips in this section will make it easier for you.

Chapter 14: Formatting and Presentation deals with the basic visual elements of an academic assignment. Do you want to know how to present your work in a professional manner? Read this chapter and find out.

So, this is how the book is going to be structured from this point on. And now – let's get down to business.

CHAPTER 3

THE FREE TOPIC

PROBABLY THE MOST important element of any academic assignment is the title. Particularly if you have to create one yourself. When you have a free choice of topic for your university essay, research paper or dissertation, you can have mixed feelings about it. On the one hand, you are excited, because you can write about whatever you want. On the other – you can be overwhelmed: 'How do I figure out what to write about?'

Now, generally there are three main rules which you have to follow:

1. Choose a narrow, focused topic
2. Pick a subject you love
3. Write about what you know

Let's look at them, one by one.

3.1. Choose a Narrow, Focused Topic

Your assignment should not be about a thousand things. It should be about *one*. So, make sure your topic is focused. Let's take this example:

The rise of the Asian Tigers (economic power in the East)

When your readers see this topic, they may ask: 'What on earth are the Asian Tigers?'

Even if they know that your essay is about the four powerful economic regions of Asia (Hong Kong, Singapore, South Korea and Taiwan), they may ask the following questions: 'What about them? Which aspect of that phenomenon are you analysing? What were the reasons for their emergence? What were the consequences? Or perhaps you want to carry out an analysis of their economic performance in the past decade?'

You cannot write everything you know about South East Asian economics. You have to narrow your topic down as much as possible.

So, how can you narrow this one down? Let's look at this example:

What were the reasons for the rise of the South Korean high-tech industry in the 1950s?

Here, we are talking about reasons and *not* consequences; South Korea and *not* Taiwan, Hong Kong or Singapore; high-tech and *not* fishing or coal and steel, and the 1950s and *not* any other time. Can you see? It's narrow. It's focused.

Let's take another example. Imagine you are writing a literature essay and exploring ideas of love in the works of Ernest Hemingway. Naturally, you will focus on love and *not* courage. On Hemingway and *not* Edgar Allan Poe or George Orwell.

This is narrow. This is focused. This is specific.

Why is this good?

Because it helps two people: you and your reader. For you, it reduces the amount of work. When you have specified in your topic what you are looking for, you only have to find that and nothing else! And your readers have a clear idea what they are going to read about.

In short, create a simple, focused question – and then answer it.

3.2. Pick a Subject You Love

This is simple and straightforward: if you love something, you will be enthusiastic about it. If you love your subject, you will happily research and write about it.

Writing about a subject simply because it is fashionable or in the news will not make you motivated. It might even make you hate writing your assignment and produce sloppy work. Writing about what you love, on the other hand, will give you ideas and make you want to find out more.

There are no bad essay topics. Especially when you have the freedom to create your own. As long as your essay answers your question, you will get marks.

3.3. Write About Something You Know

If you love your topic, you will be keen to learn about it. However, if you are not very enthusiastic about an essay and simply have a duty to do it – then write about something you know.

Learning from scratch is hard. Trust me, I know. Unless you *love* the subject.

So, if you have at least some rudimentary knowledge of an area, write about it. You can even use your previous notes or some old references, which will make things much easier.

CHAPTER 4

THE INTRODUCTION

THE INTRODUCTION IS the most important element in your academic essay, research assignment or dissertation. It's especially important for your reader. Next time you sit down to write your assignment, you must remember that your reader – even though it's your lecturer who gets paid to do it – is a busy person.

I have tried to make this book as short as possible, getting to the point without beating about the bush because you are my reader and you are also a busy person.

Your reader skims through the first page of your paper and decides whether s/he wants to read on or not. For your lecturer, it is a matter of needing to understand from the first page what you are writing about. Thus, your introduction must be very clear. It must say what the topic of your assignment is.

In general, at each stage of the writing process, but especially when writing the introduction, put yourself in the reader's shoes. Keep asking yourself the following questions: 'Is it clear enough? Will the reader know what I'm talking about? Is it still relevant to the essay question?'

4.1. What Is an Introduction?

In a nutshell, the introduction is a summary of your assignment. It must tell your reader from the beginning what you are writing about, which theories you will explore and what you are trying to prove, disprove or demonstrate. It must do this briefly and help them decide if they want to keep reading or not. Therefore, it must be packed with information, but that information must be *general*. It must be information *about* the assignment, not the assignment itself, and should summarise the content. For this reason, it is good practice to write the introduction when you have completed the essay (see **Section 4.2.** for more information).

Your introduction must refer to the following:

The object of your study

You should tell your reader what the paper is about – and you should do it in detail. Be specific. Be to the point.

The context of your study

This involves not only referring to the physical context of the object of your analysis, but also to the theoretical context. What academic approaches to the subject are known? How are they related to what your assignment is about? For example, if your essay is about the *consequences* of the Vietnam War and the majority of historians wrote about its *reasons*, their books will be of little use to you. It is important to acknowledge how the subject was approached by others.

The method of your study

Here you will need one or two sentences describing your method/s of analysis. Once again, even if your method merely involves something as simple as reading literature on the subject and looking for advantages and disadvantages or arguments for and against something, you have to specify that. After all, this is your *method*. It may seem obvious to you as you are the one who is writing the essay, but to your reader, who does not have your knowledge, it will not be that obvious.

4.2. Why Should You Write the Introduction at the End?

Once, when I was working in the learning development centre teaching students essay writing skills, a first year student came up to me and said: 'I can't start my essay. I don't know what to put in the introduction.' What I said in response was the most bizarre thing in her view and the most natural in mine.

I said: 'Don't write the introduction now. Write it at the end. Start with the middle part.'

Seems rather strange, doesn't it? The introduction goes at the beginning of the essay, so it should be written before everything else, right?

Wrong.

Unless you are really confident about what your research is all about and are absolutely sure what the outcome of your analysis is going to be, hold off with the introduction.

There are three main reasons why you should do this:

1. Writing the introduction is difficult.

It's time-consuming and you can often end up staring at a blank sheet of paper, unhappy with everything you come up with. Believe me – I've been there and done that. There's nothing more daunting and dispiriting than a blank sheet of paper.

2. You don't have all the information yet.

It's advisable to start *writing* as soon as possible even though you haven't read all the available literature on the subject. You don't have to start the actual essay – instead, you can write some notes on theory, or on research that has been carried out by others. It's good to put something down on paper – just to get the ball rolling. If you haven't started it yet, do so. It will save you a lot of time.

Naturally, you don't have all the information yet. You don't have all your references in order; you've only just finished collecting your data – but it doesn't matter! Just write something. That something can be used later, in the main body of the essay.

3. It is best to write about your most recent activity.

Just finished collecting data? Write about it! Just finished your experiment? Describe it! Just read a great article about someone who's conducted a similar study? Mention it in your 'Literature Review'. Writing about your most recent action is the easiest thing to do. You've just done it – so simply describe it to get you started while it's still fresh in your mind.

In summary, the best time to write an introduction is when you have finished writing everything else. By that time you'll have gathered your data, conducted your study and read all your research papers and books. In short – you'll be done. Now just write it all down: the topic of your study, what other researchers have done, why your study is important, the methods you have used, the question you were trying to answer and so on.

CHAPTER 5

THE LITERATURE REVIEW

WHEN THE TIME comes to write your dissertation (or sometimes even a simple research assignment), your lecturers will tell you that you need to write a literature review. As a rule, most students get confused because they've never heard of this before and naturally the unknown is scary. However, when you take a closer look, the literature review is not that scary at all. Despite the strange name, it is nothing but a critical summary of previous research on the subject. This chapter will make you familiar with this section of your study and show you that everything is simple once you know how to do it.

5.1. What Is a Literature Review?

As the title suggests, the literature review is a review (discussion combined with summary) of all the literature you can find on your topic. The literature you will be reviewing will consist of the following:

- Textbooks that describe the theory related to your topic
- Academic journal articles that describe experiments or studies related to the application of your theory
- Chapters in edited books that are related to your field of study

- Any other information such as numerical or verbal data from various reports, or relevant quotes taken from pieces of serious journalism

In short, your literature review section can also be called 'Previous Research' or 'Theoretical Background'. As simple as that.

5.2. Why Do You Need a Literature Review?

Everyone agrees that a literature review is an indispensable part of every research project, no matter how small. But why do you need one in the first place? There are three main reasons:

1. To show that you have read your books

A literature review demonstrates that you are familiar with the literature on the subject – not only the textbooks and compulsory readings, but also academic journals and conference papers which examine your subject in more detail. You should show that you've read them and are aware of what previous researchers have done.

2. To show that you know what your own research is about

It's easy to get lost in your own research and start wandering away from your topic, even if you've read **Chapters 2 and 3** and dissected/defined it as clearly as you can. Your literature review is all about getting you back on track. When you discuss previous research, you need to refer back to your own topic. When you make links between what others have done and what you're doing, you remind yourself and your reader what your paper is all about.

This may seem redundant to you. You might ask: 'Why should I write about things that are self-evident?' The answer is because they are only self-evident to *you*. You are writing about it and, as a result, always keeping the bigger picture in mind, but your reader doesn't have that picture.

3. To show that you understand potential strengths and weaknesses of the research carried out by others

Strengths and weaknesses are not objective, but relative to your research – e.g. previous researchers may have used different data and methods. You must demonstrate that you understand how your research differs from theirs.

So, how do you produce an effective literature review? You have to make it *critical*.

5.3. A Critical Literature Review

Your literature review needs special attention. Why? Because it is not just a summary of everything you've read. It's a *critical* summary.

So, how do you make it critical?

A non-critical, 'passable' literature review consists of the following parts:

- The theories you are going to use in your assignment (broad description)
- A summary of papers, chapters and articles that describe how, when and where the theories were applied in the past
- A summary of research methods that other people have used before you
- A brief description of other researchers' experiment design (participants, data used, theories tested, research methods employed)

Now, how do you transform this passable literature review into a first-class one? It needs to involve certain elements:

1. A description of the theory you are using, followed by a ***justification*** of why you chose to use this theory. You can justify your choice based on several criteria:

- The theory you are focusing on is well-established, has worked for many researchers before you, but overturned some other theory that existed for a long time. You want to reinforce the fact that the new theory works better. Moreover, you want to demonstrate that it works with your data.

- The theory is relatively new, has not been explored much yet and, consequently, there is a research gap that you are hoping to fill. You are also proving once again that it works.

- You are testing a well-established theory using new data. You are trying to find out whether it will still work.

Please note that if at the end of your study you find that something didn't work, do not despair. Try to think why the results were not as impressive as you had thought they would be – and write about it! A failed experiment is still an experiment. It is enough to write that the results are not significant to make a definite conclusion. See **Chapter 7: Analysis and Discussion** for more information on this.

2. A brief description of the studies carried out by other researchers (what you have managed to find in academic journals, book chapters and conference papers), followed by a discussion of how their findings relate to what you expect to discover during the course of your study. This should include the following:

- How your study design is similar to/different from theirs.

- How your dataset is similar to/different from theirs (e.g. maybe they collected their data in one geographical region and you collected yours in a totally different one. Or maybe their data was collected over a long period of time, and you collected your samples within one week, etc.)

- How the number of participants you used is similar to/different from other researchers' studies, or the differences between the participants' sociological profiles (see **Chapter 6: Methodology** for information on participant profiling).

For example, imagine someone did a study on work-life balance in the general population and they used more participants than you did in a similar study, which used the same process of data collection. Their study should be more representative of the larger population. However, perhaps you used fewer participants but all of them were black mothers of two or more children and aged thirty to forty – in this case, your sample would be more focused and representative of that particular social group.

- How your research method is similar to/different from theirs (maybe they chose loosely structured interviews and you used questionnaires. Maybe they used a different statistical formula, etc.) **See Chapter 6** for a more in-depth discussion on research methods.

- How will all of these similarities and differences impact on your results? Will your study have similar outcomes and findings to previous studies? Or will they be different?

Please note that these questions can differ depending on the assignment you are carrying out as well as the subject you are studying.

The main questions that you need to answer are:

What are the similarities and differences between my study and the academic study I am reviewing?

How will my study design influence my results?

The answers are very simple. S/he used A, but I used B. S/he used C and so did I. This allows you to make assumptions about whether the outcomes might be similar or different.

If you fail to produce a critical literature review and simply describe other researchers' work, your lecturer (and subsequent readers) will say: 'So what? Why are you saying this?' It sounds silly, but I will repeat one piece of advice throughout this book:

Don't imagine you're writing an academic paper. Imagine you're writing a Guide for Dummies. Explain to your reader why every little fact you mention is important and how it is relevant to your assignment.

3. An original contribution.

There is another aspect that you need to include in your literature review: your original contribution to the field of study. Of course, at undergraduate level you are not expected to make ground-breaking discoveries. Even Ph.D. students who make significant discoveries during the course of their research are rare. However, it is important to mention the following points, regardless of whether you are an undergraduate or a postgraduate student:

- How do you expect your findings to contribute to the existing theoretical framework (even if it is simply reinforcing the existing theory or 'furnishing clues' to new studies)?
- How are your data and/or method going to enrich the current body of knowledge? This can simply be the fact that no one has used this kind of data or method before.
- Consequently, what is the specific research gap you are hoping to fill?

5.4. The Structure of the Literature Review

As discussed above, your literature review must have the same structure as your entire academic paper: going *from broad to narrow*. Therefore, it follows this principle:

- From textbooks to journals
- From a description of the theory to a discussion of how the theory was applied by others
- From describing how others applied the theory to a description of how *you* will apply it

There is another important aspect of being critical: analysing how the researchers you reference have obtained their data. In your paper you should mention the specifics of their methods because the validity and reliability of a chosen methodology also matters. Please refer to **Chapter 7** for more information.

Compare your study design to those of others. Point out what the other researchers did and whether there are any potential shortcomings in their studies in relation to yours.

5.5. Examples of Good and Bad Literature Reviews

In this section, I will show you some good and bad examples from a typical literature review.

BAD:

Smith (1992) describes a sociological experiment with 200 participants. The experiment consisted of reward and punishment as incentives for work. A group of 100 people were positively reinforced by motivational coaches. The other 100 people were constantly humiliated by an actor playing an army sergeant. The experiment showed that reward was more powerful than punishment because the group which was positively reinforced performed the given tasks better.

Why is it bad?

Because it merely describes the experiment without linking it to the current study. Your reader does not understand why you mention this, why it is relevant.

Let's look at the good example.

GOOD:

Smith (1992) describes an experiment that was meant to determine whether reward or punishment was more effective to motivate people to perform tasks. His method included positive reinforcement for one group of participants by professional motivational coaches and negative reinforcement (humiliation and punishment) for the other group. During the experiment it was discovered that reward (positive reinforcement) was more effective than punishment. However, there are certain differences between the present study and that by Smith (1992).

In the present study, gaining money for performing well and losing money for performing badly is used as positive and negative reinforcement respectively. According to the study by Jameson (1989) money is not a strong motivator – praise is a stronger one. Nevertheless, the sociological profile of the participants needs to be taken into account. Jameson's study focused on office workers, who are middle class employees. The present study focuses on students, and the hypothesis is that money will be important for them as a motivator due to their social status and financial circumstances. However, this does not exclude the influence of praise and verbal positive reinforcement, which will also be taken into account.

(Please note that the researchers' names and the study design are entirely made-up).

As you can see, in the example above, I am linking the previous research with my own study and this makes me look well-read and immediately tells my readers that I know what I'm talking about. In other words, I know the differences between my study and previous studies. I also know what they have done and exactly what I am doing. This gives me credibility, allowing me to speak more confidently.

CHAPTER 6

METHODOLOGY

THE METHODOLOGY SECTION in academic writing normally refers to three components: the data, the participants and the method. The participants are not always present – only if your research involves human subjects. **Section 6.1** deals with **data collection. Section 6.2. The Participants** will discuss research ethics and the steps you need to take if you work with people. **Section 6.3. The Method** is dedicated to ways you can analyse your data and describes two research approaches: quantitative and qualitative.

6.1. The Data

Your data is anything you have collected related to your research question. It can be a set of figures that represent the changes in atmospheric pressure; it can be a collection of texts you are going to analyse, and it can also be a set of audio recordings that you have collected during a series of interviews.

There are a number of ways you can collect your data. Each one of you reading this book will have a different project to complete and therefore will probably employ a different data collection method. Therefore, the goal of this section is to explain which methods exist and the steps you can take to collect your data from your participants (or any other source, such as the public domain).

Here are some of the most popular data collection methods:

1. Literature research

This involves using both Internet and library sources (public domain texts, social media, online newspaper articles, etc.). This method is the most obvious one: you read books and journals in order to find the necessary information.

You can use this method to find all kinds of information: you may want to find descriptions of theories, theorems and scientific hypotheses, read about how they were tested and/or applied, or simply find out what Socrates said about war. The purpose of your research is not important. What matters is that you open the book and start taking notes.

Advantages

- Popular and respected in academia
- Universally applicable (great for library-based assignments when your research question can be answered by reading books instead of going 'out there' and collecting data)
- Useful for initial research – finding out the main theories and gaining general knowledge of the subject

2. Questionnaires and surveys

You create a set of questions, either with a blank space where your respondents will write their answers or with multiple-choice answers to choose from, and distribute it among your participants.

Advantages

- Multiple copies of the questionnaire can be created and distributed to as many people as you want (for example, the census is carried out in this way)

- Effective in studies which require a large number of respondents and multiple choice answers are enough – no need to elaborate on the quality of the answers
- Easy to set up (there are great online tools, and many of them are free, such as *KwikSurveys.com*)

3. Interviews

Plain and simple: you ask questions, your respondents answer them.

Advantages

- Participants are free to answer in any way they want
- Effective in qualitative research where interpretation, not calculation, of responses is important

4. Observation

You observe your participants and take notes. Also known as **ethnographic research.**

Advantages

- Useful for studying various social groups, children and animals and where observation of social interaction is paramount

5. A case study

A case study is a detailed examination of *one* phenomenon. This can be an analysis of a historical event, an organisation, a person with a particular disease, or even a translation of a text.

Advantages

- Narrowly focused, as the object of the study is clearly defined
- Universally applicable across a range of disciplines

6. Conversation analysis

Recording a conversation using an audio recorder, then transcribing it word-for-word and analysing the interaction that is taking place.

Advantages

- Allows in-depth qualitative analysis
- Useful in linguistic, sociological as well as psychological research

7. Measurements

You can measure and calculate literally anything – people's height, the average weight of all the cats in the neighbourhood, the amount of time it takes a student to solve a crossword, a person's heart rate, the daily temperature in a river and so on.

Advantages

- Effective in any type of quantitative research in the field of medicine and natural sciences

Naturally, this list is far from exhaustive. There are thousands of possible research methods – not least because the seven mentioned above can be combined and developed. They all depend on your experiment design i.e. the way you're getting your data.

To sum up, the data is the information that you've collected and compiled in one form or another in order to analyse systematically. Now, if your data is from the public domain (e.g. you have been observing cloud movements or have taken a text from an online source, like a discussion forum or a blog, whose author has made it publicly available), you can jump to **Section 6.3. The Method**. However, if, by any chance, humans are involved in your study, you need to read **Section 6.2** first.

6.2. The Participants

Your participants are the people who take part in your study. They don't have to be people you have interviewed personally – they could be friends on Facebook, whose conversations you copied and pasted into a document file to analyse how frequently they use slang. If it is not an anonymous nickname on an online forum, but a person you know, it is important that you (1) make a social profile of them and (2) observe certain research ethics procedures. Let me explain these two elements.

Profiling the participants

A profile is a description of certain elements that characterise your participants. Those elements are study-specific; in other words, they will depend on what you're trying to demonstrate by your research. However, the examples below will give you a general idea:

- Age
- Gender
- Nationality/Mother tongue
- Ethnic origin
- Social background (working/middle class, etc.)
- Habits (smoking/drinking/exercising)
- Occupation
- Education (secondary, higher, master's degree, etc.)

The list can go on and on and it's up to you to decide what to include and what to leave out.

See the table on the next page for a sample profile (it is a made-up example for a medical study).

Name	Subject 1
Age	20
Gender	Male
Smoker	No
Level of fitness	Good
Any medical conditions	No

Table 1: A sample social profile

Research ethics

There are many reasons why you should carefully observe the research ethics procedures. One of them is because you want to keep your friends. There is an anecdote among academics about a linguist who secretly recorded dinner table conversations whenever her friends came round to visit her. She got some great data out of it, even published a book, but when her friends found out and recognised themselves in the dialogues which she included in the text, they never wanted to be friends with her again.

The lesson is ***make your participants aware of what you are doing***. You do this in the following way:

1. Inform your participants of what your study is about. Sometimes this can hamper the results. For example, imagine you are analysing the features of a particular accent and a very self-conscious person with a regional accent makes an effort to speak in Standard English because they are conscious of being recorded; this will influence your data. However, you do not have to say what you are analysing precisely. You are allowed to be deliberately vague (e.g. in this particular case you could say you are analysing the features of language in the region). Be vague, but don't lie.

2. Inform your participants how you are collecting the data (observations, questionnaires, interviews, sound and video recordings, etc.)

You simply have to make sure they know. They have a right to that.

3. Do not disclose their names and other sensitive information. When mentioning your participants in your paper, call them *Subject 1, Subject 2,* etc.

4. Tell them that any data you collect from them will be stored safely.

5. Inform them verbally and in writing. Give them an ethics form to sign (see a sample ethics form below).

SAMPLE ETHICS FORM

I am conducting a research project with the aim of determining how music of certain genres affects the performance of mental tasks.

During this research experiment, I will play different genres of music and then ask the participant to solve simple numerical and verbal tests while the music is playing. The time which it takes the participant to accomplish the tasks will be measured.

The experiment will be preceded by a short questionnaire about the participant's gender, age, musical preferences, etc. and followed by a short semi-structured interview in which the participant will be encouraged to give feedback.

The experiment will last around thirty minutes.

All the information about the participant will be kept safe, secret and confidential. The personal information about age, gender, musical preferences and degree course will be included in a general table in the body of the research paper. However, the participants will never be named and no sensitive data will ever be disclosed.

I_____ (please type name) agree to the conditions above.

Signature

Date

6.3. The Research Process and Methods

In this section I will talk about the research process. First, I will write about what research is, then tell you the differences between primary and secondary research, and finally explain the differences between quantitative and qualitative research methods.

What is research?

Generally speaking, research is a process we use to find information that interests us in order to do the following:

- Learn something
- Solve a problem
- Test whether a certain idea is true
- Explore a particular area of study

Research can be divided into categories according to certain criteria. First of all, it can be primary or secondary, according to how the researcher obtains his/her data; secondly, it can be quantitative or qualitative, depending on how the researcher analyses the data. I will explain these differences in the tables below.

Table 2. Primary and secondary research

Primary research
Involves first-hand observations and investigation. For example, a physicist or chemist experimenting in the lab, a psychologist observing a group of children, or a literature scholar analysing a novel by Charles Dickens are all engaging in primary research.

Secondary research
Involves examining and evaluating studies made by other researchers. Secondary research can be carried out through reading textbooks, journals, academic articles as well as pieces of serious journalism.

It must be said that academic research projects often involve both primary and secondary research.

When it comes to grouping research according to research methods, generally speaking, it is divided into quantitative and qualitative research. The table below summarises the two.

Quantitative research	Qualitative research
View on reality	
Reality is objective. There can only be *one* view of the world.	Reality is subjective (it is subject to interpretation). The researcher's view of the world depends on the theory that s/he has employed.
Bias	
The research is value-free and unbiased.	The research is biased and value-laden.
Relationship between the researcher and the object of study	
The researcher is independent from the object of study.	The researcher interacts with the object of his/her study.
Data examination	
The data is examined objectively, without interpreting it.	Interpretation of data is allowed.

Where is it used?	
It is used predominantly in natural and life sciences.	It is used predominantly in humanities and social sciences.
Research methods	
Statistics, experiments, measurements and questionnaires are used.	Text analysis, interpretation, historical analysis, interviews and conversation analysis are used.

Table 3. Quantitative and qualitative research

6.4. Research-Related Dangers

When devising your research method, you have to be aware of certain research-related dangers. Please bear these in mind:

1. Assimilating with the object of your study

This often happens during ethnographic research – you assimilate with the group and stop noticing its peculiarities, taking it for granted. As a result, your research can lose its perceptive edge. Moreover, sometimes, instead of describing a certain phenomenon, you become an evaluative journalist. This happens when you get so involved with the study that you start analysing your feelings and reactions to the study as well as giving opinions about it instead of describing it in a detached manner. This is something to be wary of.

2. The 'Microphone Paradox'

I experienced this while conducting my study on the Birmingham accent. I was analysing its features and how it changes over time by recording older and younger speakers and comparing their speech. However, I had a problem: one of the older speakers switched from her regional accent to a more standard form of English from time to time when I recorded her. This could be explained by the fact that the Birmingham accent is somewhat stigmatised, so she wanted to sound more 'standard' and 'proper'. I wanted an authentic recording, but got a fusion of standard and regional.

The 'Microphone Paradox' can even occur without the microphone present. What I mean is that your participants may give you the responses they think you expect to hear and, as a result, the data you collect may not be genuine. So, it's extremely important to design your research in a way that allows you to collect the best, most authentic data.

3. Research ethics

Your participants must be aware of everything you're doing and you must have their consent. Talk about research ethics to your lecturer each time your study involves people.

CHAPTER 7

ANALYSIS AND DISCUSSION

I DECIDED TO combine these two sections of an academic assignment into one chapter. In fact, researchers often choose to combine the two because analysis and discussion are closely intertwined. The analysis section is merely a description of your results and findings (*what* happened), whereas the discussion section is where you try to explain the reasons for those results (*why* it happened this way and not the other, making links to your literature review).

7.1. Analysis

This section will be brief. It will describe the essence of your analysis section.

So, what should you include in your analysis?

This is simple: you need to tell your reader what you found when you looked at your data and present it in some way – either as a table, a graph, or some extracts of the text you've been working with.

I cannot tell you much about presenting the data because each of you will be working on a different project with different datasets. What I can tell you, however, is that your analysis, unlike the other parts of your assignment, should be purely descriptive. You should present the data as it stands in the following way:

- In summary, this is what my results are.
- I have some figures that you can see in the graph.
- I have some responses to the survey that you can see summarised in the table.

Nothing more, nothing less.

The evaluative commentary you are making on your results is called the ***Discussion***.

7.2. Discussion

What should the discussion section include?

Your discussion is the section in which you comment upon your experiment, your participants, your data and your results. You also try to explain *why* the results are similar to, or different from, those of other researchers.

Ideally, your discussion should contain the following elements (please note that the examples below are entirely made-up):

1. Explanation of how your findings are related to what other researchers have found

a) The results may vary because of similarities and differences between the ***participants***. This must include comments on the number of participants and their sociological profiles. I have given an example of this below:

Smith (1993) used only men in his study on competitiveness. Moreover, his participants were all male middle-class office workers. The present study used working-class women, and therefore, since the results are different, it is possible that either the social class or gender of the participants could have had an impact.

b) The results may vary because of similarities or differences in the ***data you collected and that collected by*** *other researchers, as well as the study design.* The following example illustrates this:

It has been found that while listening to classical music, the participants were able to perform mental tasks better than when listening to jazz or rock music (those genres scored second and third respectively in terms of their efficiency for concentration). These findings are in line with Robinson's (1994) study in which he also used classical music, jazz and blues. Classical music scored much higher than either blues or jazz (second and third place respectively). However, it must be noted that Robinson does not specify which pieces he played. Moreover, he does not specify whether the pieces he played were instrumental or had lyrics. In the present study all pieces were instrumental. This could be the potential reason why jazz came third in Robinson's research and second in the present study.

c) The results may vary due to similarities and differences in the **methods used**. The following example shows how this is presented:

The results of the present study are different from Johnson's (1989) findings, but he used questionnaires which limit the possibility to expand on the answer. However, in this study interviews with open-ended ended questions were used, which allowed the participants to be more reflective and elaborate their answers.

2. Explanation of why the results are not exactly the same as expected in the hypothesis

The words above are somewhat misleading. Your results do not have to echo your hypothesis – in fact, it is perfectly fine if they do disprove it, or prove it only partially. However, the emphasis here is on the explanation as to *why* the hypothesis could not be proven (or disproved) *perfectly*. By this I mean the need to acknowledge your limitations.

Top four reasons why you should admit your weaknesses

When you're writing an academic paper – no matter whether it's a first year essay or a Ph.D. thesis, it is very important to acknowledge your limitations.

It is a must for every researcher to recognise the weak points in their work and clearly acknowledge them in their writing, so that the reader would have no doubts about the limitations of the research.

So, where can you find weak points in your academic work? Some areas to look at are listed below:

- Weaknesses of the theory (because no theory is perfect)
- Weaknesses and deficiencies of the data (because your data can only be representative of a small percentage of all the data available in the world)
- Weaknesses of the research methods (because every research method has its limitations)

Here are the top four reasons why you should acknowledge your limitations:

Reason #1: Your lecturer will like it.

Yes, acknowledging your weaknesses and limitations is a sign of a mature researcher and a professional. Doing this will earn you points. Being over-confident and cocky will not.

Reason #2: No theory is perfect.

A perfect one-size-fits-all theory is called reality. It is just as useless as a map with a one-to-one scale.

The benefit of any theory lies in the fact that it depicts a limited view of reality from a single viewpoint, excluding multiple minor factors. It allows the researcher to analyse and generalise, but, of course, the limited view is a drawback at the same time.

However, you have to finish your paper some time, so you can't combine all the theories in the world and write about your topic forever. Just choose a theory, acknowledge its limitations and stick to it.

Reason #3: There is no such thing as perfect data.

No matter how hard you try to make your data maximally representative and useful for your study, there will always be limitations to it.

Your sample will always be too small. The number of respondents to your questionnaire will never represent the entire population. The number of people you interview needs to be reasonably small so you can type up and analyse their responses in the given time-frame.

Even the number of books and journals you have read will not be large enough because you just can't read them all.

This has to be admitted.

Reason #4: There is no perfect research method.

Whatever technique you choose – statistical analysis (quantitative methods) or reading carefully, looking for notable features and comparing what you find against an existing theoretical framework (qualitative research), it is usually one and not the other.

However, if you decide to combine several different methods, it may mean that one method is not representative enough, or there is a potential for error and you want to re-check something.

In short – make it clear that your research is limited and there is no limit to perfection. Even if your data is brilliant.

After all, research is all about bridging one knowledge gap and creating another.

A conclusion can be drawn from the points mentioned above: your results do not perfectly prove or disprove your hypothesis because your data, method or experiment design will always be imperfect. All you have to do is acknowledge that imperfection.

Once again, I repeat that this is never a problem in academia. In fact, there is a legend in scientific circles about the experiments Thomas Edison carried out during the process of inventing the light bulb. Edison tried ten thousand different materials that he thought would burn inside the bulb, but each time the experiment failed. He was asked by one of his colleagues: 'Aren't you discouraged by failure? You've already failed ten thousand times!' Edison's reply was: 'On the contrary – I've succeeded ten thousand times! I've found ten thousand materials that don't work!'

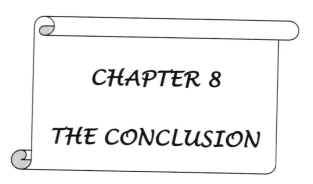

CHAPTER 8

THE CONCLUSION

SO, YOU'VE DONE IT – you've finished your main body and planned how you will summarise it in your introduction. Now you've only got one little bit left – the conclusion. So how do you do it?

This chapter will explain what your conclusion should contain.

As I have already mentioned in this book, all academic writing (and the majority of written communication as well as public speeches) can be summed up in three parts:

1. Say what you're going to say (introduction)
2. Say it (main body)
3. Say what you've just said (conclusion)

The conclusion is nothing but a summary of your assignment. It should have the following elements:

1. Restate what the essay/research report/dissertation was about. Mention the topic. Draw the reader's attention to the narrow focus of the research question and the data sample (and profiles of your participants where applicable).

2. Briefly describe the methods used, the data which was analysed and, if applicable, who the participants were.

3. Summarise the results.

4. Recount how they correspond to previous research in the subject area. Do they prove it? Disprove it? Why are your results the same, similar or different?

5. Remember – only write about *your data* and *your research*. Often inexperienced students tend to jump to conclusions that are full of sweeping generalisations. They tend to say that if something was the case with their data, it is therefore universally applicable and works each time. They tend to judge the entire population by the results of a small sample of participants.

You need to avoid this. Your conclusions should only concern your data and how it fits within the theoretical framework you are using. Do not make assumptions about the world based on your limited analysis.

6. Once again – I cannot emphasise it enough! – acknowledge your limitations. At least say that they exist; there is no need to be specific in the conclusion. Say that they have 'implications for new research'.

In short, describe each section of your assignment in one or two sentences and your conclusion is ready.

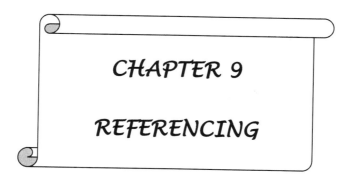

CHAPTER 9

REFERENCING

THIS CHAPTER DEALS with the nitty-gritty of academic writing – referencing. This part of the assignment is something that many students, especially first years, can't stand. I can totally relate to it: you are not allowed to express your own opinion, and even for the basic facts like 'the Earth is round' you need to acknowledge who wrote about this and refer to his or her book. Boring and annoying!

All right, the above example is an exaggeration – but this is the way things are in academia. Every thought that is not your own (and in the beginning of your studies this is almost every thought in your essay apart from your own conclusions that you base on other people's research) needs to be referenced.

This chapter will tackle the three most important questions about referencing:

1. What is referencing?
2. Why do we need referencing?
3. Which referencing systems are used in academia?

9.1. What Is Referencing?

Imagine you are talking to your friends and you want to report something a mutual friend said the day before. How do you do it? You say: 'Guess what Michael told me yesterday! He said quitting his old job was the best thing he's ever done in his life.'

Now, this idea is not yours. You may even think that it was foolish of Michael to quit his job. However, you distance yourself from the issue – you mention Michael's name and thus make it clear that the idea is not yours. You are reporting that idea and Michael's words but they do not become your own. This is how referencing works.

Referencing is a way of presenting someone else's ideas: you indicate the author of the idea, the year s/he expressed it and the publication (book, article, letter, etc.) in which the idea appeared. It is a way of telling the reader that the idea does not belong to you but that you know this information.

9.2. Why Do We Need Referencing?

So, why do you need to indicate that the idea belongs to someone else – and do it in so much detail, too?

The first reason is simple: because it is fair. It is a way of showing respect to the author who came up with the idea.

You certainly wouldn't be happy if someone stole the essay that you had been labouring on for weeks and handed it in as their own. Perhaps you are so protective of your work that you would freak out if you saw one sentence in someone else's work that looked similar to something you had written. I can tell you that all academics are like that. They are possessive of their writing and so proud of it that they want to be acknowledged each time someone refers to their ideas – even if only in passing.

The second reason is that failing to reference is an academic offence. If you are caught stealing someone else's thoughts, the consequences may be severe. You will definitely receive a zero mark and will have to redo your assignment; under certain conditions, you may even be expelled (especially if you steal another student's work). You reference because it is better to be safe than sorry.

9.3. Main Referencing Systems

The four largest referencing systems are: Harvard, Oxford (also known as the Footnote system), MHRA and APA.

As I do not know which system your university uses (and often different systems are used in different faculties), I will simply give you web links where you can find them. Please note that the links were correct at the time of publication. More links to different referencing and study guides can be found on the websites of *The Lecture Room* and *First Year Counts*.

The Harvard System

University of New South Wales, Australia:

http://www.lc.unsw.edu.au/onlib/ref.html
http://www.lc.unsw.edu.au/onlib/pdf/harvard.pdf

Anglia Ruskin University:

http://libweb.anglia.ac.uk/referencing/harvard.htm
http://libweb.anglia.ac.uk/referencing/files/Harvard_refer encing_2011.pdf

Leeds Metropolitan University

http://skillsforlearning.leedsmet.ac.uk/Quote_Unquote.pdf

The Footnote System

University of Gloucester

http://resources.glos.ac.uk/shareddata/dms/9F4295CDBC D42A0399BA0A2A6E688835.pdf

University of New South Wales, Australia:

http://www.lc.unsw.edu.au/onlib/refbib.html
http://www.lc.unsw.edu.au/onlib/pdf/biblio.pdf

The MHRA System

Cardiff University:

http://www.cardiff.ac.uk/insrv/resources/guides/but028.pdf

The Official Modern Humanities Research Association Website:

http://www.mhra.org.uk/

The APA System

Birmingham City University:

http://library.bcu.ac.uk/APA.pdf

University of Southern Queensland, Australia:

http://www.usq.edu.au/library/help/referencing/apa

In addition, the University of Leeds provides a comprehensive guide to less-known reference systems, like Vancouver and OSCOLA:

http://library.leeds.ac.uk/skills-referencing

CHAPTER 10

WHAT ABOUT EXAMS?

THIS CHAPTER DEALS with exam questions. In particular, it explains how to answer essay-style exam questions that are often encountered in the humanities, social sciences, business studies, economics and, a bit less often, in natural and life sciences.

Essay-style exam questions look just like normal assignment questions (see **Chapter 2**). The only difference is that you have the entire term to write an essay, but only one or two hours to write an exam.

See below for an analysis of the advantages and disadvantages of exams and essays.

ESSAYS

Advantages

1. A lot of time to complete them, plenty of time for reflection and analysis, and you can use spell-check.

2. You are allowed to use books, journals, the Internet and any other resources you need.

3. You know the question in advance.

4. You can give it to someone else to read and get feedback.

5. You can consult your lecturer and your friends during the writing process.

6. Essays can also be written in groups.

Disadvantages

1. Referencing is a pain in the neck.

2. You have to keep backup copies everywhere in case you lose your USB stick or your computer crashes.

3. You have to read much more for an essay than for an exam. Your sources must be many and varied.

EXAMS

Advantages

1. They are quick. You learn the information, write it down and then you can forget about it!

2. No need to reference (usually). Although, if it is an open book exam, you might need to reference.

Disadvantages

1. *Time is short.* There may not be enough time to proofread or even to finish answering the questions.

2. You have to carry out a lot of research in advance, keep it all in your head and get it down on paper in, usually, less than an hour per question.

3. You don't know the questions in advance, so either you are revising day and night or guessing what will come up.

4. You have to be quick when answering the questions. Almost this entire chapter is dedicated to time management. How do you answer an essay question in a quick and efficient manner, from the introduction to the conclusion, with enough time to proofread your answers? Read on to find out!

Exam writing strategies

The process of writing an exam is very similar to writing an essay. The key elements in this 'race against time' are focus, strategy and timing.

An essay-style exam can be tackled by following these steps:

1. Research.

In an ideal world, your lecturer would give you access to exam questions from previous years. Lecturers are not likely to write a new exam paper every year – instead, it is much more likely that they will only change the questions slightly and add one or two new ones.

If you have access to past exam papers, you will have a chance to prepare some answers in advance. Otherwise, go over the lecture slides and materials. Identify the main topics – those most discussed in class. It is likely that each exam question will correspond to one lecture topic.

After you know, more or less, what the questions will be, you can start researching. Follow the same process you would for an essay. First, read general texts – textbooks as well as the lecture slides. Next, start reading academic journals and more specialised articles. Make a note of those journals – although you do not need to reference anything in exam papers, it will certainly gain you extra points if you mention specialist studies of the subject area in the exam paper!

Do not try to learn all the topics. You will have to answer two or three questions out of eight to ten possible ones. Focus on four to five topics at most. Select the topics you found most interesting.

2. Practise.

Prepare your answers in advance. Don't try to pull it off on the day of the exam. Look at past papers and practise writing answers to some of the questions in the form of an essay. Time yourself. Keep practising.

Copy your lecture notes – write them out by hand or type them. This will make you more engaged in the process than just reading them.

Prepare draft outlines for your answers. Practise now because you will have to write an outline in the exam, too!

3. Read the questions *very* carefully.

They might ask for exactly the same thing as last year, but there can also be a different angle on each of the questions.

4. Determine the order in which you will approach the questions.

This is up to you – you could start with Question 1, the most difficult one, or the topic you know best.

5. Identify the object, context and method.

Look for the three elements of the question: the object of the study, the context of the study and the method of the study. Then start answering the question.

Just as you would when writing an essay, you need to acknowledge the limitations of your theories and remember that there is always more than one point of view. Provide a balanced opinion.

6. Prepare an outline.

As with a normal essay, prepare an outline for your answer to the exam question. Plan the structure and the organisation of your response. This will help you to focus your answer and present your ideas more coherently.

It is also a good time to remember relevant information from your reading and write strong, substantiated arguments rather than just vague statements.

Don't spend too much time on the introduction or the conclusion. What really matters in exams are logical arguments and showing a connection between the pieces of knowledge in the main body.

7. Answer the questions.

Keep to the point. Don't spend too much time on background information. Keep it simple – just focus on the question. Keep in mind the object, the context and the method. The rest is irrelevant.

Don't think for too long about how to phrase things better. Speed is more important than style.

8. Manage your time.

Allow yourself enough time for answering all the questions. It is better to write the outline for each question at the beginning so that it's easier for you to plan your answers later.

Leave some time at the end for revision and proof-reading. Sometimes, when you're in a hurry, mistakes can creep in unnoticed. Contrary to what many students think, grammar, clarity, proper punctuation and correct word choice also count in exams. So, try to make sure that you are writing in correct English.

CHAPTER 11

THE WRITING PROCESS

WRITING IS HARD work. Just ask any writer. Even writing this book wasn't easy.

In this chapter, I will share some tips that I used for my assignments at university, as well as while writing this book. I will tell you how to make the writing process much easier.

The key to all writing is **careful planning**. You need to know what will happen paragraph after paragraph. All writers follow this advice – even those writing fiction. If you think that J.K. Rowling wrote all seven Harry Potter books just by winging it, you are seriously mistaken. No successful writer has even written anything merely from inspiration. Every book was planned paragraph by paragraph and chapter by chapter.

You should do the same when writing an academic assignment. Here's how you can do it.

Planning and structuring your assignment

1. Start with the essay question

Write the question at the top of your sheet and *always* keep it in front of you and in mind. Every sentence of your essay must contribute to the main purpose of your assignment – answering the question.

2. Brainstorm

Write down *all* of the possible ideas for the main body of your assignment that come to your mind.

Yes, *all* of them. Later, you will be able to discard those that don't seem good enough.

3. Write an outline

Write down what will appear in separate sections of your assignment. For example, take a look at the outline of an essay on the benefits and drawbacks of electric cars below.

What are the advantages and disadvantages for the economy and the environment of having only electric cars in the future?

1. Introduction. Electric cars – potential future transport, could be economically beneficial. Research how fast this industry is growing; research the main debates around this issue.

2. Arguments for:

   a. Fewer emissions, more environmentally-friendly. Research how much CO_2 cars are currently emitting globally.

   b. New jobs created in the green economy, new products and services. Find out more about the economic benefit; find some figures!

3. Arguments against:

   a. Electricity for cars can still be produced in 'unclean' ways – nuclear or coal, oil and gas.

   b. People working in the fuel-powered car sector can become jobless. Research!

   c. Potentially high cost of training and retraining specialists.

4. Conclusion. Potentially a good idea, but cars alone would not change the environmental situation. A substantial change of the entire system – especially electricity production – is needed.

4. Research your subject

This can be done before you start brainstorming or outlining, but it is better to do it afterwards, when you have some ideas about your topic.

Read all you can find related to your subject and the ideas you came up with during the brainstorming and outlining process. For more information on the research process, see **Chapter 13: Writing Tips**, especially **Section 13.1. The Researcher's Point of View.**

5. Start writing

Even better – start writing early. The most difficult thing is putting words down on the page.

You have to start doing that immediately.

When you are reading a textbook or research article, take notes.

When you think of a link between two facts, write it down immediately.

'Chopping dead wood' off your writing is easy. It's much more difficult to add words, thinking: 'Oh, when will I reach the word count?!'

6. Use transitional words and phrases

These are words like *first of all, secondly, finally, moreover, furthermore, however, nevertheless, also, on the other hand, in conclusion, etc.*

These are the words that will make your writing coherent. Use them well!

7. How do you write a paragraph?

This question is not as easy to answer as it seems. A paragraph, in essence, is a mini-essay. Therefore, it must have its own introduction, main body and conclusion.

One paragraph should contain one idea. Your paragraphs should be structured to include:

1. A topic sentence

2. An explanation of the topic sentence

3. A piece of evidence that supports the topic sentence. Here you can do the following:

- Give examples to illustrate your idea.
- Provide a quotation or reference that supports your topic statement.
- Anticipate counterarguments and respond to them.
- Offer another perspective to the idea (to provide a balanced opinion).

4. An explanation of the significance of that evidence (why it is important or relevant)

Please see an example of a paragraph structured in this way below. The numbers mark the following elements:

(1) The introductory sentence

(2) A reference and a quote that elaborates the argument

(3) Logical conclusion from what the referenced author says, explaining why what is said above is relevant

(4) Coming back to today's context; linking to the essay question

(5) Responding to potential counterarguments

(6) The concluding sentence

The essay question:

Using relevant theory (e.g. motivation), discuss the extent to which the principles of scientific management are relevant to organisations in the early 21st century.

The paragraph

*It is necessary to be familiar with the historical context of scientific management theory **(1)**. Merriman (2004) states that at the end of the nineteenth and beginning of the twentieth century the USA was experiencing an immigration boom. Many people left Europe seeking a better life in the United States. They wanted to escape poverty or persecution. However, the life they found in the New World was also a hard one. They 'depended on their labor for survival' (Merriman, 2004, p. 836) **(2)**. Furthermore, according to Merriman (2004) they had 'harsh working conditions' and 'low wages' (p. 837). Many of these people were from poor regions like southern Italy. Many of them were Jews from Eastern Europe. Therefore, they spoke poor English, or did not speak it at all (Merriman, 2004). Taylor's scientific management was to be applied to these people, since, as common sense would suggest, they could only carry out simple, unskilled work, and splitting the task into subtasks made it easy to train the workforce **(3)**. However, nowadays the situation is really different **(4)**. Many more people are becoming skilled workers and English is a global language, too. Hence, Taylor's principles are not that relevant. But, of course, it should not be forgotten that unskilled labour still exists **(5)**. Therefore, the relevance of Frederick Taylor's scientific management depends on the context in which those principles are applied **(6)**.*

8. Write the introduction at the end

It's a good idea to write your essay in the following sequence: *Main Body – Conclusion – Introduction.* See **Chapter 4: Introduction** for more details.

9. Stick to the rules

Read the requirements for the essay carefully. If it says Harvard referencing system, only use that system. If it says 2,000 words, do not wander from that number by more than ten per cent. If it says 12 point Times New Roman font, use that font.

Play by the rules. These things matter.

CHAPTER 12

THE LANGUAGE OF ACADEMIA

SOME PEOPLE SAY that if you can speak well, you can write well. I would like to agree with this statement, but, unfortunately, in academia it isn't that straightforward. Sometimes academic English can sound like a foreign language – and the ones to blame for this are the academics themselves.

There are several features of academic English that, as a university student, I found annoying – for instance, long, complicated sentences, and 'big words' that authors appear to use to sound intelligent and well-educated. These do nothing but confuse the readers – even if they are native speakers – and send them running for the dictionary. There are also some rules that academics obey out of tradition, for example, impersonal language and the overuse of the passive voice. In this chapter, I will discuss these features and tell you how to write in a style that will earn you points.

Young researchers (particularly undergraduates) fail to follow them and, as a result, reduce their chances of obtaining a higher grade. These rules might seem counter-intuitive to you, but I learned them during my university experience and they always worked for me. I'll discuss them later in this chapter.

So, what is it that makes academic English so particular? There are six main features:

1) Overuse of the passive voice
2) Impersonal language and writing in the third person

73

3) Big words and long sentences

4) 'Doubtful' language

5) Specific jargon and vocabulary

6) Formal register

Let's analyse them all, one by one.

1. Overuse of the Passive Voice

Journalists often use the passive voice because 'it is the way we do it'; the use of it by novelists and bloggers is frowned upon. So, what should an academic writer do, especially if s/he is only an undergraduate or a master's student and is not yet in the position to write the way s/he wants?

It is true that many academics use the passive voice out of tradition *(the data were analysed; the experiment was conducted).* However, it is not the rule of thumb any more. When I read current academic papers, I see phrases like 'I gathered the data' or 'in this paper, I examine the effects of...'

Nevertheless, to be on the safe side, it is best to consult your lecturer about this.

2. Impersonal Language

For some reason, lecturers do not like seeing the word 'I' in assignments – especially followed by the word 'think'. I understand the latter: your opinion must be backed up by facts. You cannot come to a conclusion without evidence. But what is wrong with using the word 'I' if it is really *you* who has conducted the study?

In the first and, to some extent, the second year of university, you are taught to back up your claims with evidence from the literature. You are taught to take other people's knowledge, summarise it and answer the question that is given to you. Therefore, it is natural that during the initial stages you will have much less freedom and the word 'I' will be rarely seen in your work. However, as you become involved in more and more independent projects, you will be able to use the first person more often, because you will begin to gather and analyse your own data.

Nevertheless, talk to your lecturers for each of the modules and find out what they prefer. Impersonal language *(This essay aims to explore...)* is often used, although it is clear that not the essay but the student aims to explore the subject. In some universities the tradition is to use not 'I' but 'we'.

3. 'Big Words' and Long Sentences

This section is all about 'eschewing obfuscation'. This phrase is a joke among writers; it means 'eliminating ambiguity', or, in plain English, 'making it clear'.

It may seem like the use of long-winded sentences and words that can stretch across Luxembourg is a sign of an educated mind. To me, however, it makes things less clear for the reader. Do you really think that the reader wants to go one paragraph back to make a link between two long sentences? Do you think they will think less of you if they don't have to rush for the nearest dictionary? I really doubt that.

Short words are powerful. You shouldn't ignore long ones altogether, but don't overdo it.

This is the area where you shouldn't blindly copy what academics do. Some of them just like showing off their huge vocabulary. Follow the KISS principle: Keep It Short and Simple. Don't write for your professor. Write for your grandma.

4. 'Doubtful' Language

Before I begin analysing this feature, I have to say that doubt is something that academic writing is soaked in. There is no space whatsoever for absolute statements and a know-it-all attitude. The only time you are allowed to speak with certainty is when you analyse and discuss your data. However, you must remember that your data sample has its limitations and you shouldn't make general sweeping statements about the wider world based only on your sample (for more discussion on this subject, see **Chapter 7: Analysis and Discussion**).

In academic writing, being 'doubtful' means the following:

I am certain that some things are the case when it comes to my data, methods and research design. However, there are other data samples, methods and research designs out there, and if I had used them, my study might have worked better, worse or not worked at all.

When you're writing an academic assignment, you cannot have all your arguments in favour of a certain case. At least one argument should be against it in order for you to provide a 'balanced opinion'. Often you are explicitly asked to provide an analysis of the pros and cons or to 'discuss' an issue, which means that you have to give a certain number of arguments proving that something is the case, then say 'on the other hand' and give a number of arguments proving that it is *not* the case.

This 'balanced structure' is the one that academics follow throughout their careers. In general, a good researcher is one who knows the limitations of his/her work and can acknowledge them.

There are certain words and sentence structures that you should include in your academic writing. These are the words that demonstrate your 'awareness of limitations':

- Modal verbs (*can, could, may, might*, etc.)
- Certain adjectives and adverbs expressing a degree of probability (*possible (-ly), probable (-ly), potential (-ly), plausible (-ly)*, etc.)
- Other phrases (*to an extent, to a (certain) degree, somewhat*)

Let's look at an example:

*The results of the present study demonstrate that the participants who were smokers performed the physical exercises they were given with lesser efficiency and lower levels of energy than the non-smoking participants did. This **suggests** that smoking does negatively influence physical performance – at least **to a certain degree**. It must be noted, however, that smoking is not the only factor, and the results depend on the individual habits of the participants. For example, **it is possible that** a smoker who exercises regularly and has a healthy diet will perform better than a non-smoker who does not exercise at all.*

Looking at the example above, it is useful to bear in mind two things:

a) You have to speak confidently about your results (*what* they are).

b) You need to express doubts about your interpretation of the results (*why* they are like that).

Be aware that individual lecturers may have their own ideas about appropriate academic language. Therefore, it's a good idea to **consult your lecturer** and even ask what style s/he prefers. Keep collaborating with academic staff. Ask your lecturer as much as you can. You will only benefit from it.

5. Specific Vocabulary

This section mainly focuses on the vocabulary found in assignment titles and briefs and is therefore more applicable to set assignments rather than to those with a free topic.

There are certain words that you find in assignment briefs which can be quite hard to understand. They are vague and it is often hard to figure out what they mean.

Here are some of the most popular ones:

Account for

Analyse

Compare (and contrast)
Critically evaluate
Discuss
Enumerate
Evaluate
Justify
Outline

They are explained below, one by one:

Account for

Explain something; clarify; give reasons for it. Please note that it is different from 'give an account of' which is more like 'describe in detail'.

Analyse

Study something in detail. Break it into its main components (parts) or characteristics and explain how they relate to each other.

Compare (and contrast)

Take two (sometimes more) objects – or ideas, or methods or whatever you have been asked to compare – and identify what they have in common. Write about it. Then find what their differences are – and describe them too. Summarise the similarities and the differences at the end.

Critically evaluate

Weigh arguments for and against something, assessing all of the evidence. Based on this, decide which opinions, theories, models or items are preferable.

Discuss

This one is my favourite. It is used in essay questions quite often. It means that you need to carefully examine and analyse the *object of your study* and then present all the pros and cons regarding any issues or items involved. This requires meticulous work.

The main point is to present both sides – the pros and the cons. This shows that you *know* both sides. It does not ask you to agree with opposing opinions – you have to merely show that you are familiar with at least two points of view.

Enumerate

This word has the word 'number' hidden in it. In other words, it asks you to number something, or to make a list of something. You should recount them one by one.

Evaluate

When asked to evaluate, you are expected to present a careful appraisal of the object of your study, emphasising both its advantages and limitations. Evaluation implies that you need to base your arguments regarding the benefits and drawbacks on the literature you've read. Your conclusions should also be based on evidence from the literature and not on your personal opinion.

Justify

When you are instructed to justify your answer, you must prove, or show grounds for, decisions. In such an answer, you should present your evidence in a convincing form.

The main point is to convince. You do not have to convince your reader that you are right – it is enough to show that there is logic in your words and that your ideas are coherent and stem from logical reasoning based on facts.

Outline

Present the main features of the object of your study and emphasise their structure. The main point is to *explain*.

Of course, this list is far from exhaustive and there are many more keywords that are used in essay titles. However, based on my academic and professional experience I can say that those listed above are used most frequently.

(The author thanks the University of New South Wales http://www.unsw.edu.au/ and Frostburg State University http://www.frostburg.edu/ for the materials on their websites that he used to prepare this section.)

6. Formal Register

It is important to understand that the language of your academic assignment is not the language of a text message or a Facebook chat. There are certain features that make the language of academic assignments formal.

No contractions

This book is written in conversational style and I do allow myself some informality – I use contractions (*don't, won't*, etc.) However, in an academic piece, this is not acceptable. Always use the full form: *do not, is not, they will, it has/it is*, etc.

No slang

It was bare good when Johnson (1995) tore apart Smith's (1989) method and results. That was sick, man, I'm tellin' ya!

Oh, how I would love to read something like that if I were a lecturer! It would certainly make my day and I would take that student out for lunch – if only to praise his/her originality and richness of vocabulary, as well as to explain the differences between communication in the professional environment and outside of university.

I know that most of you will just laugh and say: 'no one writes like that'. It's true, I am exaggerating. But there are many people who write exactly the way they speak. It is important to understand that written and spoken English are often very different languages.

Use the first person sparingly.
Be careful with the passive voice.

Both features are a matter of perspective and each lecturer might have his or her own opinion regarding them. Do not forget to collaborate with your lecturer if you have any doubts. This has a double benefit: (1) you will get to know each other better and s/he will see that you are interested and will have a higher opinion of you; (2) you will get corrections and feedback, and, consequently, a chance to improve your grades!

Use Standard English. No regionalisms.

In London, it's a *sarnie*; in the Midlands, it's a *bap*; in the North West, it's a *buttie*; in Glasgow, it's a *piece*.

In Standard English, it's a sandwich.

You might not encounter this word very often in academic writing, but you get the idea. As a linguist, I love the English language for its diversity. As an academic writer, I think that we need to have some order.

Keep to the standard in university essays and exam papers.

Also, if you're an international student, you might want to use British or American English. Each has its own vocabulary and spelling system. Please be consistent – use either one or the other!

Oh, yes – and *no* text/chat lingo either!

I wud lyk 2 dscryb de political dvlpmnt of Gr8 Britn...

Ok, I am exaggerating again. But I need to make it clear: do not write anything in shorthand. Your essays reflect your professionalism. Writing an essay is like doing a task at work: if you do it in a messy way, you face the consequences.

I don't want anyone to repeat the mistake of a 13-year-old girl from Scotland who, in 2003, wrote her English essay in text language 'because it's easier than normal English'. The world that George Orwell was describing is not yet entirely upon us and most people would like to keep the English language as it is without switching to Textspeak/Newspeak. Your lecturers are among those people.

Avoid phrasal verbs

Do not *rule out* the possibility of failure – *eliminate* it. Your participant did not *freak out* – they were *agitated*.

The use of phrasal verbs makes your work look like magazine journalism – informal and somewhat slapstick by the standards of academic writing. I have nothing against magazine journalism, but leave it to the magazines. Using overly formal language is not that bad, especially in writing. You may not speak that way, but it will certainly help you if you adopt this form in your academic writing.

Use credible references

This one is related to **Chapter 9: References**. The most important aspect of your reference list is that it should contain credible sources. By *credible* I mean the following:

a) The author should not be someone from the street but a respected professional in their field – either an academic or a practising professional/expert.

b) The publication should have been issued by a credible organisation. By this I mean a publishing house, a university or a limited company. It can be published online, e.g. in an electronic journal or on the website of the organisation, but it cannot be a private blog or a Wikipedia article. In other words, it cannot be a source that everyone and anyone can edit.

Avoid idioms

When doing your research, you may sometimes find yourself *between the devil and the deep blue sea*. You may be worried that the tasks you will ask your participants to perform might *not be their cup of tea* and that a bad mark for this assignment will *throw your chances of getting a first out the window*.

However, when it comes to putting your thoughts on paper, you should avoid idiomatic expressions. The language should be plainer, stricter and more conservative, even if you are studying creative writing or literature. Your text should sound professional, educated and formal.

7. Explain Acronyms and Abbreviations

I am sure that you know what UNESCO, the RSPCA and NAFTA stand for – especially since you're the one who is writing an essay about them. However, I would like you to explain them to your reader, too!

Never assume your reader knows.

Imagine that your lecturer is uneducated and needs everything explained. This is the only way to go about it.

8. Do not make grammatical mistakes

Use your spell checker and your head. Revise your work. See **Chapter 13: Writing Tips** for more information on this one.

CHAPTER 13

WRITING TIPS

IN THIS CHAPTER, I will give you some simple tips that will make the writing process easier for you. When approaching an academic assignment, each student should have three personalities in himself or herself: the Researcher, the Grammarian and the Writer. Here are some writing tips from each of the three:

13.1. The Researcher's Point of View

From the researcher's point of view, academic writing is first and foremost looking for the right information, assembling it and keeping it safe. Therefore, what you should be looking for in your assignment as a researcher is, first and foremost, information.

Now, before we talk about the accuracy of information, it is important to know where to look for it. Here are some tips:

1. Start on Wikipedia. Yes, despite what I said above, it's a good place to start. Just do not put it in your reference list. Wikipedia is a wonderful online tool for getting information, but, unfortunately, it can be edited by anyone and, as a result, terrible inaccuracies can creep into otherwise brilliant articles. Thus, it is good for getting *general knowledge* on the subject of your research, but then you need to move onto more approved sources.

Like, for example, the list of references that the author of the Wikipedia article used. Yes, those folks also do reference their work. Often their sources are extremely good: academic books, online journal articles, websites of serious organisations, etc. It's worth checking them out.

2. Next, move on to textbooks. Textbooks are valid academic sources, but they have one great disadvantage: they are too general. Usually the information you need is concentrated in one chapter and the rest of the book is simply irrelevant. Read that chapter and go online for more.

3. Use online academic journals. My favourite place to look for them is Google Scholar. Your university also has an electronic library full of academic articles from the journals that your institution subscribes to. There are thousands upon thousands of them in there.

If you cannot access the journal you are looking for online for free, you can look it up in print. Your university library keeps printed copies of many journals as well. Journals describe specific cases when the theory was tested or applied.

4. Then move on to websites as well as online and offline publications of serious organisations (like governmental ones or businesses, or even a blog run by a public figure, etc.) Your sources will also depend on your research question.

5. You can also use email correspondence with someone who has authority in your field of study. This could be an academic, a manager of a company, a politician, or an expert in a certain area.

6. Finally, move on to serious newspaper and magazine articles. Journalists also need to research and acknowledge their sources. A false statement in the press can cost the publisher a lot of money. Naturally, with these sources you have to be critical and take them with a pinch of salt; after all, an article in *The Times* is not equal to an article in *The Daily Fool* tabloid. And even *The Times* journalists' writing should be examined with a critical eye.

Why did I give the tips in this order?

Because the order of writing an assignment is always moving from general to specific.

In addition to these literature-based research tips, here are some general reminders of what you need to do in order to make your research project as professional as you can:

1. Acknowledge your limitations. You need to remember that there's no perfect theory; no dataset is too big; and your participants only represent one particular social group.

2. If your research involves human subjects, observe research ethics and do not disclose any sensitive information about your participants (see **Chapter 6: Methodology** for more on the topic).

3. Don't forget to link each section to your research question. Treat all sections as mini-essays; write a short conclusion at the end of each section, explaining *why* what you've written is important and relevant.

4. Make notes while you're reading. Found interesting points in that textbook, chapter or article? Write them down immediately!

5. Keep records of all your references. Names, dates of publication, titles, website URLs, etc. As soon as you get hold of something, note down the full reference (see **Chapter 9: Referencing**). It will be hard to track down later. Keep that list safe.

6. **Back it up.** Your work is your baby. Losing it is painful. Keep several copies: on your computer, on a USB stick, e-mail it to yourself, save it as a PDF because Word documents might become corrupted, etc. If you do not have a PDF converter on your computer, there is an excellent resource online: http://convert.neevia.com/pdfconvert/. You can also download free Word to PDF conversion software – there is plenty of choice on the Internet.

13.2. The Grammarian's Point of View

I don't like being a grammarian. I don't like teaching people how to spell or punctuate. But I'm thinking about your readers – and so should you.

It is very likely that your reader (in this instance, your lecturer) is someone who uses 'proper English'. Consequently, they can't stand poor English. When you are writing, you should always think about your readers – because you are writing for them. You should aim to give them clearly expressed thoughts, good ideas, logical reasoning – and beautiful, fluent language. Grammatical and spelling errors can be like a slap in the face to them. They will lose you marks.

This is the only reason why this section is important: **to keep your marks intact.**

So, let's begin.

Mistakes that make you look stupid

These are the basic grammatical and spelling mistakes that your spell checker might not detect, but your reader will. You should avoid them.

Their/there/they're

The difference between these is the following:

Their = belonging to them (*The children are playing with their toys* – the toys belong to the children.)

There = not here (*Look over **there**. **There** are many job opportunities in the city.*)

They're = they are (*Look at the results! **They're** astonishing!*)

Look at this sentence to see the difference between the three: ***They're there*** with ***their*** *friends.*

Your/you're

Your = belonging to you (*Congratulations on finishing **your** studies!*)

You're = you are (*If you keep procrastinating, **you're** going to fail!*)

Lose/loose

Lose (verb) = opposite of *to find*, to misplace (*You will **lose** marks if you do not obey essay writing rules!*)

Loose (adjective) = not tight (*Those clothes are quite **loose**.*)

Quiet/quite

Quiet (adjective) = not loud, silent (*You are being very **quiet** today. Is anything the matter?*)

Quite (adverb) = rather (*The data set is **quite** small.*)

No/know

No = opposite of yes (*There is **no** proof that your theory is correct.*)

Know (verb) = to be aware of; to have knowledge of (*I **know** that the experiment will be successful – I've done it before.*)

It's/its

Its = belonging to it (*The questionnaire has **its** limits.*)

It's = it is (***It's** obvious that the data set is not large enough.*)

Would of/would have

This is another common error. The best way to avoid it is to think what this verbal construction is made of. It is made of the modal verb *would* + a verb in the Present Perfect tense *(have been, have done)*. Since you would not normally write

~~I of been~~ or ~~you of done,~~ the construction is always **would have done, could have been, should have analysed.**

Whose/who's

Whose is a pronoun. It means *belonging to someone.* (***Whose*** *book is it?*)
Who's is the short form of *who is.* (***Who's*** *on duty today?*)

Less/fewer

Less is used with uncountable nouns, like milk, bread, interest or energy. (*During the experiment, the machine consumed* ***less electricity*** *than we had thought it would.*)
Fewer is used with countable nouns like light bulbs, ideas, participants, etc. (*We used* ***fewer participants*** *in the study than the previous researchers.*)

Effect/affect

Effect is a noun. It means *impact.* (*This study will examine* ***the effect*** *of globalisation on business practices in Poland.*)
Affect is a verb. To affect = to have an effect (*Let us see how the new drug* ***will affect*** *the patients' conditions.*)

Then/than

Then is used for time and sequence. Then = not now, later (*The data were summarised and* ***then*** *exported into the table.*)
Than is used for comparison. (*The number of participants was lower* ***than*** *was expected.*)

The apostrophe rules

This is my personal pet hate and a topic that has been discussed many times before. But, as a writer, and as an involuntary grammarian, I must remind my readers of these simple rules:

The apostrophe is used in many situations; however, the two most common rules are the following ones: when we identify the owner and when we shorten words.

The owner rule

When there is only one owner whose name ends in 's', you place an apostrophe and another 's' after it.

The pencil belongs to James, so it is ***James's*** *pencil.*

If there is more than one owner and the plural ends in 's', you just place an apostrophe after that final 's'.

For instance, if the house belongs to the Smith family, it is ***the Smiths' house.***

If the name of the owner ends in another letter, then you put an apostrophe and an 's'.

For example, if a car belongs to John it's ***John's car.***

The same applies if the owner is in the plural and the plural ends in another letter:

Men's toilets – because the toilets are for men and thus 'belong to them'.

The shortening rule

This one is even simpler. When words are shortened, the apostrophe takes the place of the missing letter(s).

Do not = don't

Cannot = can't

Will not = won't

You are = you're

They are = they're

Would not = wouldn't

I have = I've

She is = she's

It is or it has = it's

Who is or who has = who's

13.3. The Writer's Point of View

As a writer, I must remind my readers that the process of writing is inevitably linked to the process of rewriting. As I have said before, writing is hard work. This section explains what this phrase really means:

1. There is no such thing as a perfect first draft. You will have to rewrite your essays, research reports and dissertations.

So, you will have to get good at ***rewriting***!

2. Do not rewrite or edit anything before you complete the first draft. Yes, I mean it. Do not edit anything. When you open the unfinished document, start from where you stopped last time. Otherwise you might perfect your first paragraph or chapter but never write the second one.

3. After you finish your first draft, let it lie for a day or two. If you have no time and the deadline is fast approaching, leave if for several hours and go and do something else. Then come back to it and have a look with fresh eyes.

4. It's OK to get sick and tired of writing. Take a break.

5. Don't spend all day at the computer or working on a sheet of paper. Write in bursts of 30 minutes and then do something else for five minutes (ideally a physical task). However, if you feel like writing for a longer period, you're welcome to do it. Everybody is different.

6. Never leave the sheet of paper blank. Write something. Brainstorm, write whatever ideas on the topic come to mind, set out a basic structure, or think what kind of arguments your work might contain. Do anything, just please don't leave a blank sheet.

7. Persevere. Writing is not an easy task. I am trying to help you by writing this book, but I can't write your work for you. You have to push yourself a little. Just write and see those letters connect and form words, words form sentences, sentences form paragraphs, etc.

8. Good writers also read. Read as much as you can – books, academic papers, newspaper articles and anything you can find related to your subject. Read to boost your vocabulary; read to see how academic papers are structured and in what style they are written; read to enhance your knowledge. Reading does pay off.

9. Carry a notebook everywhere. You never know when and where a great idea might strike you.

10. Do not try too hard to write like an academic. By all means, use a thesaurus in order not to repeat a word, but refrain from overusing 'big words' and long sentences. Being clear pays off much more. Imagine that your grandma will be reading this. Write it in a way she would understand. Do not be informal, just be clear.

I got my first with my grandma in mind.

11. Writers write, that's what they do. But they also go for walks, work out in the gym and visit the swimming pool. Don't forget about physical activity – it will help you unwind and relax. It also stimulates creativity.

12. Have fun and keep writing!

CHAPTER 14

FORMATTING AND PRESENTATION

FLIP THE PAGES back and look at this book. Do not *read* it, just *look* at it. Look at how the chapter names are placed in the centre of the page, how the paragraphs are indented, how the margins are of the same size on every page and how the text is justified from both sides.

This is called *formatting*.

This element of your academic writing is just as important as anything I've mentioned previously. Why? Because your work must look professional. You also get marks for it. It is worth about 5 per cent, which could be the difference between a 2:1 and a first.

So, how do you format your work? There are many ways and guidelines differ from university to university (sometimes even from lecturer to lecturer), but there are some general rules to follow:

1. Uniform fonts

Sometimes the computer is set by default to one particular font which you don't really like. Make sure that it doesn't accidentally jump to that font when you hit the Enter key.

2. No fancy fonts

Plain, simple ones like the one used in this book (Cambria), Times, or Arial are the best ones. Don't experiment – unusual fonts are not professional and can be difficult to read. Font size – between 12 and 14 points.

3. At least one-inch margins

Even better to leave 3 cm (1.25 inch). Your lecturers will be making comments in the margins, so leave them plenty of space. If you intend to bind your work, leave additional space on the left-hand side.

4. At least 1.5 point line spacing

Once again, make it easy to read. Have mercy on your lecturer's eyes.

5. Page numbers

Even if your work is stapled firmly, after being handled by many pairs of hands it can come apart. Do not make your lecturer suffer, trying to figure out which page comes after which.

6. Sections

If your work is longer than 2000 words, it is advisable to divide it into sections. In fact, you can add sections to an assignment of any length – just name them 'Introduction', 'Arguments for', 'Arguments against', 'Discussion', 'Conclusion', or according to whatever they contain. This will make it easier for your reader to navigate your work.

Read some academic papers to see how they are structured and follow that structure.

7. A table of contents

Add a table of contents, listing all the sections with the page numbers (especially if your work is longer than ten pages, or 2000 words). Guide your reader – especially if that reader is your lecturer who has sixty (or sometimes 600) other essays to read for this module and, to be honest, is quite tired of reading them.

8. The cover page

Add a simple cover page with your student number, the module code and the title of the work (requirements may differ from subject to subject). Your university should have guidelines – refer to them or ask your lecturer to find out which specific formatting rules you need to follow.

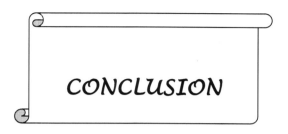

CONCLUSION

SO, YOU'VE REACHED the end of this book. I hope I've taught you something useful and reminded you of some of the things you already know.

So, what is the next step?

Apply all you've learnt. First, have a look at your old assignments. Do they contain the elements they should contain? Is everything you say somehow related to the title of the assignment? Do you make explicit links between the sections? Do you go from general to specific?

Now think about the assignment you have to do and make sure everything you write is coherent, relevant and correct.

Start right now.

Plot it. Brainstorm. Make notes while you're reading. Plan the sections of your assignment. What will they contain? How will they be structured? If in doubt, refer back to this book.

Oh yes – and one more thing. Be a real academic. Don't just believe what I write. Check other sources. Talk to your lecturer. Read other books.

Write your killer essay! Get that first!

Have fun and keep writing!

Vlad Mackevic.

CAMP UK

10/2012

THE ULTIMATE POST-2012 UNIVERSITY SURVIVAL GUIDE (UK EDITION)

VLAD MACKEVIC

DEAR READER,

THESE PAGES OF MY BOOK CONTAIN A BONUS – AN EXTRACT FROM ANOTHER BOOK OF MINE CALLED *CAMP UK 10/2012. THE ULTIMATE POST-2012 UNIVERSITY SURVIVAL GUIDE.*

THIS BOOK (WHICH IS DUE TO BE LAUNCHED IN DECEMBER 2012) IS ABOUT BECOMING A PROFESSIONAL FROM THE FIRST DAYS OF THE FIRST YEAR. IT IS ABOUT MAKING THE MOST OF YOUR TIME AT UNIVERSITY AND GAINING VALUABLE SKILLS FOR WORK AND FOR LIFE. I HOPE YOU WILL ENJOY THIS SAMPLE.

IF YOU LIKE IT, YOU CAN FIND THE BOOK ON AMAZON.CO.UK AND MY WEBSITE: WWW.FIRSTYEARCOUNTS.COM.

THANK YOU AND ENJOY READING!

VLAD MACKEVIC

UNIVERSITIES OFFER SO MUCH! YOU JUST NEED TO KNOW WHERE TO GO TO FIND IT!

2012 IS A TOUGH YEAR FOR BOTH THOSE WHO ARE JUST STARTING UNIVERSITY AND THOSE ABOUT TO GRADUATE. JOBS ARE SCARCE, COMPETITION IS IMMENSE. ALL EMPLOYERS DEMAND WORK EXPERIENCE, BUT WHERE DO YOU GET IT? HOW DO YOU STAND OUT FROM ANOTHER GUY OR GIRL WHO WILL ALSO GET A 2:1?

THE ANSWER IS SIMPLE: TAKE THE BULL BY THE HORNS! GONE ARE THE TIMES WHEN IT WAS ENOUGH TO BE A GRADUATE TO LAND A GOOD JOB. MUCH MORE IS NEEDED NOW. MOREOVER, WITH TUITION FEES AS THEY ARE, IT'S IMPORTANT TO ENSURE THAT STUDENTS ARE GETTING THEIR MONEY'S WORTH FROM UNIVERSITY!

THIS BOOK PROVIDES ANSWERS TO ALL THE BURNING QUESTIONS. IT TEACHES YOU HOW TO:

- MAKE THE MOST OF YOUR TIME AT UNIVERSITY

- GAIN WORK EXPERIENCE WITHOUT EVER LEAVING THE CAMPUS

- ACQUIRE THE SKILLS THAT ARE ESSENTIAL AT EVERY WORKPLACE AND PRESENT THEM ON YOUR CV WITH MAXIMUM EFFECT

- CREATE A COMMUNITY OF FRIENDS, CLIENTS AND SUPPORTERS AROUND YOU AS A PROFESSIONAL FROM THE FIRST DAY OF THE FIRST YEAR

- GET YOUR MONEY'S WORTH OUT OF EACH DAY OF YOUR UNIVERSITY EXPERIENCE.

A MUST FOR EVERY STUDENT!

INTRODUCTION

ATTEN-TION!

Say goodbye to your old life. Forget everything that you've learnt before because life starts anew here. Welcome to Camp UK 10/2012. If you thought it was going to be easy, think again.

After so many years of hard work, sleepless nights spent revising for your A-Levels, preparation and worrying, you've finally made it to university. You are probably looking forward to your new life, possibly away from home. You could be feeling a little nervous. Whatever your expectations are, prepare to be surprised.

I've written this book in order to surprise you, perhaps even to shock you, to make you think and to help you. The information it contains will blow your mind! I have to tell you right from the start that you are reading it at your own risk. But it's a risk that is totally worth taking.

This book tells you the truth about university and about the real world out there. It tells you about the challenges that modern students face and about ways to overcome them.

Let's start with the bad stuff. In the past (it can already be called 'distant'), it was enough to walk into a company waving a piece of paper that proved you had listened to lectures for three years and obtained your degree and you would be hired almost immediately. Having a degree was the key to a skilled job.

Nowadays, things have changed. Modern students and graduates are facing four main challenges during and after their university lives:

1. Too many graduates and too few jobs

Let's face it: everyone has a degree nowadays. Universities offer courses in everything – from accounting to Zulu Studies – and hundreds of thousands of young people with a Bachelor's degree enter the job market every year.

Moreover, competition among graduates with good degrees is tough: in 2011, one in seven graduates was awarded a first class and over half of those finishing university ended up with a 2:1.

In the meantime, the number of vacancies is not keeping up with the number of graduates. Every year, a number of graduates remain unemployed, have to do unpaid work for the sake of work experience (which not everyone can afford) or stay in jobs where they cannot realise their full potential. The competition for good jobs is fierce: a single vacancy can receive up to 200 applications, and in areas like law or financial services the number is double or even triple.

So, all new students entering university in 2012, as well as those who started earlier, face the same problem: how do you stand out from the crowd? How do you distinguish yourself from your neighbour who is also going to get a 2:1? How do you attract an employer who filters applications based only on academic achievement?

2. Too many unfilled vacancies

Isn't it a paradox? So many graduates, so few jobs – and still, employers struggle to fill these vacancies. How is it even possible? Why is this happening?

The answer is very simple: graduates fail to match the employers' requirements. According to a recent survey carried out by the Association of Graduate Recruiters, employers' demands become stricter as competition toughens. At the same time, students often perform well academically but fail on 'soft skills' such as efficient written and spoken communication, teamwork, interpersonal skills, active on-the-job learning and work ethic.

The biggest problem of modern students and graduates is not unemployment, but unemployability caused by the lack of necessary skills.

There are many ways to get 'soft skills', and I will talk about them in detail here. One of the ways is by having *any* job, paid or unpaid. By merely being in the world of work, you can pick up basic skills and contacts – networking seems to be one of the best ways to learn what's available. Moreover, you can develop these skills by performing well academically and getting involved in university life beside your studies.

But how do you get that first job? And even if you do, will this bartender/waitress/sales associate experience really matter when it comes to a serious job interview? How do you *make it matter*? And how do you acquire those 'soft skills' for the time when you will need them?

This leads to a third challenge.

3. Every employer wants work experience

Yes, almost all employers say that they will only consider applicants for graduate and even placement positions who already have some work experience – ideally, it should also be relevant.

It's easy to explain why this is the case. First of all, recruiters want serious, committed individuals who are not afraid of hard work, are willing to learn new skills and already know what it means to have a job and to show up every day, even if you don't feel like getting up.

If this is fine with you, then the following questions arise:

- How do you get work experience while you're still an undergraduate?

3

- How do you get *serious* work experience that extends beyond the range of so-called 'usual student jobs'?
- How do you draw benefit from every little bit of work experience you have got?

4. University is becoming more and more expensive

Education costs are soaring. The 2012 generation will have to pay £9,000 per year in tuition fees and, as a result, will accumulate substantial debt by the time they graduate.

The problems are obvious: how do you make the most out of your time at university? How do you make every hour of every day count towards your degree, towards your employability, and towards your future? How do you make sure that you get your money's worth?

I will tell you the truth: university offers a lot for your tuition fees. You just need to know where to find what you need and how to make best use of it.

Naturally, the current economic and educational climate is not the easiest one, both for those entering university this year and those who are already studying. The problems I have listed above are likely to be the same in the years to come.

The good news is that you are holding the answers in your hands. I have written this book because I would like to share my own experience – what I have observed in myself and my classmates whilst at university – with you. I want to tell you what I wish I had known when I was an undergraduate. A lot of advice I am giving in this book came to me one way or another long after my graduation – all because I started too late.

Your generation cannot afford to start too late. You have to take things seriously right from the start.

The advice I give in this book will help you gain an advantage and compete even with older graduates. It will help you become a professional from the first day of the first year. This book answers the main questions all current undergraduate students are asking:

- How do I stand out from the crowd of graduates when everyone has a good degree and some work experience?
- How do I obtain valuable transferable skills that all employers demand?
- How do I gain some serious work experience that extends beyond the usual student jobs?
- How do I get my money's worth out of university? What am I really paying for? How do I use every opportunity to develop personally, academically and professionally so that my time is spent in the most efficient manner?

I am ready to give you the answers. I have written this book with a view to helping you become more employable and prepared for real life than you could have ever imagined. However, before we start, I would like to point something out. This book is entirely subjective. It is largely based on my personal experience. I cannot guarantee that having read it you will immediately get a great job. What I can say, however, is that those who do nothing, get nowhere.

So, let's start with the basics – what you need to do to get where you want to be.

CHAPTER 1

THE BIGGEST LIE IN YOUR (UNIVERSITY) LIFE

This is one of those moments you will remember for the rest of your life. It is celebration time and all your family members are calling to congratulate you. After years of hard work, revision, and probably one or two sleepless nights, you've *finally made it to university.*

Congratulations once again! You arrive on campus, hardly able to believe your luck – three years full of adventures that will change your life lie ahead of you. You are excited. You are proud. You are slightly worried. You brace yourself for a new life.

And then it happens.

As soon as the rumbling engine of your parents' car fades away in the distance, as soon as you step into the crowd, ready to plunge into your new life headfirst – you are told something that is probably the biggest lie you will ever hear during your university life.

This lie sounds too good for you to start doubting it – and this is where its danger lies. It is capable of turning an optimistic, determined, enthusiastic fresher into a lazy couch potato and opportunity waster.

This lie is: *the first year of university doesn't count.*

One of the reasons why I have written this book is because I want to counter this lie and protect all students from the danger it poses.

It is a dangerous lie because... it's partially true. I agree that the first year of university sometimes feels like a gap year you never intended to take – especially after all the A-level related pressure. However, even a gap year can be spent in numerous ways: some just choose to go travelling and make their gap year one big party; others go to the developing world and help to build a school or a hospital in a local village. It's up to you how you spend your time.

Yes, the grades of your first year do not count towards your final grade at the end of your final year (although currently it is being planned to revolutionise the system by introducing new 'report cards' and redesigning degree classification systems altogether). However, too many freshers are tricked into believing that they can just have fun, do the bare minimum needed to pass the first year and watch television and play sports in all the time that remains.

I have to disappoint you – life's not that easy anymore. This lifestyle might have been acceptable ten years ago, but now the situation is too desperate to continue living like that.

The first year *does count* and its significance is paramount. The most obvious reason why it counts is because it is *your time*. Imagine someone told you that one year of your life is worthless; the effort you make during that time also counts for nothing. How would this make you feel? How would you react? I can bet you'd challenge this person because your time is worth *everything* to you. You wouldn't be at university unless you thought it was worth your time. You are also reading this book because you think it's worth investing your time in it.

Moreover, imagine this situation:

You are applying for a summer internship at the end of your first year or you start looking for a work placement at the start of your second year.

Most probably, your employer will want to see your academic credentials, especially if you have little or no relevant work experience. What are you going to tell your future boss?

'Hey, look here, I got 54% average in the first year, but in the second year I promise to have no less than 68%?'

No one's going to fall for that.

Therefore, unless you have decided not to do an internship or gain any work experience at all (which is the worst thing you can do), the grades of your first year *do* count.

Moreover, even though your first year grades don't count towards your academic progress (which is also likely to change in the future, looking at the current education reforms), it is still worth making more effort in the first year because many second year modules are based on what you learn in your first year. In other words, the better you perform in the beginning, the less effort you will have to make later on. If you need more information on how to obtain higher grades, without snapping from overwork in the process, you can find great tips in my book *From Confusion to Conclusion: How to Write a First-Class Essay*. Free samples of the book as well as related articles can be downloaded from my website:

www.FirstYearCounts.com

as well as from the website I write for:

www.TheLectureRoom.co.uk

Yet, there's no need to study to the point of exhaustion. The best way is to find a healthy balance between your studies and extra-curricular activities. I will talk a lot about those in this book. Since the grades of the first year are not nearly as important for your academic progress as those of the second or the final year, I strongly advise you to spend as much time as you can allow developing non-academic skills by 'doing a lot of stuff' – engaging in extra-curricular activities with clubs and societies and gaining serious work experience.

In summary, your first year does count. It counts towards your studies, your skills, your work experience and, above all, your future. I have written this book to show you how to *make it count* and gain maximum advantage, taking all the benefits you can from your university life, starting from the first day of the first year. Read on and find out how to do it!

ABOUT THE AUTHOR

VLAD MACKEVIC is an author entrepreneur, an academic writing expert and an employability consultant. He writes fiction for the soul (under the pen-name Roy Eynhallow) and non-fiction for the mind. He graduated from Aston University, Birmingham with a First Class degree in International Relations and English Language. During his professional life, he has worked as an academic writing mentor and a communications officer. This book was written to sum up Vlad's professional and academic knowledge and to share it with you for your benefit and enjoyment.

Connect to Vlad online:

Websites
www.FirstYearCounts.com
www.TheLectureRoom.co.uk

For Fiction (pen name Roy Eynhallow)
www.EynhallowBooks.com

Facebook
https://www.facebook.com/First.year.counts

Twitter
http://twitter.com/Vlad_Mackevic
http://twitter.com/EynhalowBooks

LinkedIn
http://www.linkedin.com/in/vladmackevic

18820637R00069

Printed in Great Britain
by Amazon